Manifesting the Glory

Tony Kemp

Tony Kemp
P.O. Box 3366
Quincy, IL 62305
www.tonykemp.com

Brewer Publishing
www.tdbrewer.com

ISBN: 978-1-942260-02-8

For global distribution, printed in the United States of America.

Contents

CHAPTER 1:

What is the Glory of God?

The GLORY OF GOD is the ESSENCE of WHO and WHAT HE IS in HIS FULLNESS. The GLORY OF GOD is the totality of all that the FATHER, SON, and HOLY SPIRIT are in knowledge, wisdom, understanding, character, and ability.

> **"The eyes of the Lord are in every place, Keeping watch on the evil and the good." Proverbs 15:3 (NKJV)**

The Word of God says that the Lord is all-knowing or omniscient.

> **"To the only wise GOD our SAVIOR, be glory and majesty, dominion and power, both now and ever. Amen." Jude 1:25 (KJV)**

So, the Lord is the all-wise God and understands all things.

"Where can I go from your Spirit? Or where can I flee from your presence? If I ascend into heaven, You are there; If I make my bed in hell, behold, You are there. If I take the wings of the morning And dwell in the uttermost parts of the sea, Even there Your hand shall lead me. And Your right hand shall hold me." Psalms 39: 7-10 (NKJV)

So, the Lord is omnipresent or everywhere present at the same time.

"Because it is written, Be ye holy; for I am holy." 1 Peter 1:16 (KJV)

So, the Lord and HIS character are HOLY.

In the beginning God created the heaven and the earth. Genesis 1:1 (KJV)

The scripture calls God the Creator of all things. So, God is All-Mighty!

"For with God nothing shall be impossible." Luke 1:37 (KJV)

God is able to do ALL things.

The apostle, Paul, prays this prayer in the book of Ephesians.

"I am asking that the God of our Lord Jesus Christ, the Father of Glory, may give to you the spirit of wisdom and revelation in the knowledge of Him." Ephesians 1:17 (NKJV)

God is the <u>Father of Glory</u>.

"But we speak the wisdom of God in a mystery, the hidden wisdom which God ordained before the ages for our glory, which none of the rulers of this age knew; for had they known, they would not have crucified the Lord of Glory." 1 Corinthians 2: 7-8 (NKJV)

Here, the apostle Paul points out that none of the princes of this world knew the FATHER'S plan, because if they had known, they would not have crucified the Lord of Glory, Jesus.

"If you are reproached for the name of Christ, blessed are you, for the Spirit of glory and of God rests upon you. On their part He is blasphemed, but on your part He is glorified." 1 Peter 4:14 (NKJV)

Here the Word of the Lord says the Holy Spirit is the SPIRIT of GOD'S's GLORY. So, the GLORY refers to the PERSON OF GOD. That is the FATHER, SON, and HOLY SPIRIT.

"But as many as received Him, to them He gave the right to become children of God, to those who believe in His name: who were born, not of blood, nor of the will of the flesh, nor of the will of man, but of God." John 1:12-13 (NKJV)

When you receive Jesus, you become a <u>child</u> of the FATHER because you have been born again.

> **"But as many as received Him, to them gave He power to become the sons of God, even to them that believe on His name:" John 1:12 (KJV)**

When you receive Jesus, you become a <u>son</u> of God.

> **"There was a man of the Pharisees named Nicodemus, a ruler of the Jews. This man came to Jesus by night and said to him, 'Rabbi, we know that You are a teacher come from God; for no one can do these signs that You do unless God is with him.'**
>
> **Jesus answered and said to him, 'Most assuredly, I say to you, unless one is born again, he cannot see the kingdom of God.'**
>
> **Nicodemus said to Him, 'How can a man be born when he is old? Can he enter a second time into his mother's womb and be born?'**
>
> **Jesus answered, 'Most assuredly, I say to you, unless one is born of water and the Spirit, he cannot enter the kingdom of God. That which is born of the flesh is flesh, and that which is born of the spirit is spirit. Do not marvel that I said to you, you must be born again. The wind blows where it wishes, and you hear the sound of it, but cannot tell where it comes from and**

where it goes. So is everyone who is born of the Spirit.'" John 3: 1-8 (NKJV)

When you receive Jesus, you are <u>born again</u> by the Holy Spirit. The Spirit of God is the Spirit of Glory. Your mind is not born again. Your head is not born again. Your soul is not born again. It is your *human spirit* that is born again by the Spirit of God, by virtue of your repentance from sin and your faith in Jesus Christ. If you are born again by repentance and faith, and the Spirit of God comes into your heart, that means GOD'S's GLORY enters your spirit through faith in Jesus Christ. That means Jesus, the Lord of Glory, lives within your heart (your human spirit)!

"To them God willed to make known what are the riches of the glory of this mystery among the Gentiles: which is Christ in you, the hope of glory." Colossians 1:27 (NKJV)

"For in him dwells all the fullness of the Godhead bodily; and you are complete in Him, who is the head of all principality and power." Colossians 2: 9-10 (NKJV)

All the fullness of the Godhead lived in the person of Jesus Christ! Jesus, living in your human spirit becomes the possibility of you realizing the fullness of God's glory!

"But if the Spirit of Him who raised Jesus dwells in you, He who raised Christ from the dead will also give life to your mortal bodies

through His Spirit who dwells in you." Romans 8:11 (NKJV)

If you are in Christ Jesus, then all that God is lives in you. So, the fullness of God's Glory is actually residing in your spirit!

> **"One Lord, one faith, one baptism; one God and Father of all, who is above all, and through all, and in you all." Ephesians 4:5-6 (NKJV)**

The FATHER actually lives in your heart. The FATHER OF GLORY lives in your spirit by virtue of your FAITH in the LORD JESUS!

> **"The Spirit of truth, whom the world cannot receive, because it neither sees Him nor knows Him; but you know Him, for He dwells with you and will be in you." John 14:17 (NKJV)**

Here Jesus spoke to His disciples about the Holy Spirit, saying that the world cannot receive the Spirit of Truth, because they do not know HIM, but they, His disciples, know the Holy Spirit. HE is with them, but HE shall also be in them. HE is with you, but HE is also in you!

The SPIRIT of GLORY, the LORD of GLORY, and the FATHER of GLORY are all living in your heart, by virtue of your faith in the Word of God and in the person of Jesus!

The Lord, the God of Glory, who sits on the throne, governing the heavens and the earth, by the Spirit of HIS SON, JESUS, is also living within you. The very Glory of God is living within you because of Jesus!

The first key is to know that the God of Glory, who sits on the throne, actually lives within you, and you have access to all God is by the Word of the Lord through your personal relationship with Jesus!

CHAPTER 2:

Revelation of the Father, Part 1

"The Spirit you received does not make you slaves, so that you live in fear again; rather, the Spirit you received brought about your adoption to sonship. And by Him we cry, "Abba, Father." Romans 8:15 (NIV)

Apostle Paul tells you that you did not receive the spirit of a slave, but you received the Spirit of God, and you have been adopted as a child of God. Because of that, the Holy Spirit causes you to cry out, "Abba Father." Because of your repentance from sin, and your faith in Jesus, your human spirit is born again by the Word of the Lord and the Holy Spirit. Now God is your Father.

Abba means *Daddy*. It is what a beloved child calls his or her father.

Abba is the intimate affectionate name for Daddy God. It is the name that every child of God can depend upon. When your relationship with God is as your Daddy, it means that Abba meets all of your needs. You are like an infant, baby, or child that does nothing but receives from his or her Daddy. Daddy God is your ORIGINATOR, NOURISHER, and PROTECTOR.

> **"having predestined us to adoption as sons by Jesus Christ to Himself, according to the good pleasure of His will," Ephesians 1:5 (NKJV)**

It is because of Jesus that the Father adopted you as a son or as a daughter. It was the good pleasure of His will. In addition to God being your Daddy, He is also your Father. The Greek word for *Father* is *pater*. It is a reference to the Father having a full-grown son who is now able to take responsibility and receive his inheritance through Jesus Christ.

> **"In him also we have obtained an inheritance, being predestined according to the purpose of Him who works all things according to the counsel of His will," Ephesians 1:11 (NKJV)**

In Christ, you have obtained an inheritance. In the ministry of Daddy God, you have the *pouring out of blessings*. In the ministry of the Father, you have the *building up* of the sons and daughters of God through the teaching of Jesus.

When you minister by the grace of Daddy God, it is *for the people*. When you minister by the grace of the Father God, it is what you're doing *with people* to help them *develop into spiritual maturity*.

When you minister the blessing of Daddy God, it is to *meet the needs* of the people. When you minister the blessing of Father God, it is *to equip the sons and daughters* to act responsibly and to do the works of Christ.

The Hebrew name for *son* is *banah*, and it means to build the family name. When you minister by the grace of Daddy God, this scripture applies.

> **"And my God shall supply all your need according to His riches in glory by Christ Jesus." Philippians 4:19 (NKJV)**

In the grace of Daddy God, you see a *ministry model*. It is what the Lord is doing for people. In the ministry of Father God, you see a *leadership model*, where there is the creation and raising of sons and daughters to adulthood. Then those full-grown sons and daughters give birth and raise other children for faith in Jesus.

> **"And He Himself gave some to be apostles, some prophets, some evangelists, and some pastors and teachers," Ephesians 4:11 (NKJV)**

Jesus gave the church apostles, prophets, evangelists, pastors, and teachers. These individuals are servants of the Lord, and they serve the body of Christ in a *ministry identity*.

> **"But as many as received Him, to them He gave the right to become children of God, to**

those who believe in His name:" John 1:12 (NKJV)

You are sons of God by virtue of your faith in Christ Jesus. So, a person can also minister out of their *personal identity* as a son or daughter of God. In your ministry identity, you share with people the *anointing of Jesus*.

In your eternal identity as a son or daughter of God, you share with people the *Glory of Jesus*.

"For it was fitting for Him, for whom are all things and by whom are all things, in bringing many sons to glory, to make the captain of their salvation perfect through sufferings." Hebrews 2:10 (NKJV)

Paul says that it is the Father's intention to bring many sons into His Glory. That means that you can minister out of your gifting or the anointing in your ministry identity. Or, you can minister out of the Glory of Jesus in your eternal identity as a son or daughter of the Father God.

The primary way that the Lord Jesus ministered was out of HIS sonship. In Hebrew history, when a father saw his son come to maturity, he took him to the gate of the city and made an announcement. "This is my son," he would say. In other words, from this day forward, whenever you do business with my son, you do business with me.

"And the Holy Spirit descended in bodily form like a dove upon Him, and a voice from heaven

which said, 'You are My beloved Son; in You I am well pleased.'" Luke 3:22 (NKJV)

When the Lord Jesus was baptized in the water, the heavens opened, and the Holy Spirit descended. The Father said this is the Son of My love and in whom I find delight. In other words, the Father was saying this: This is My son. From now on, when you do business with My Son, you do business with Me. If you have a good relationship with My Son, you have a good relationship with Me. If you have a great relationship with My Son, you have a great relationship with Me.Simply put, God was saying when you deal with My Son, you deal with Me. My Son represents Me, the Father, accurately, thoroughly, and completely. Notice when Jesus walks in His sonship, the glory of God falls! This truth is illustrated on the mountain of Transfiguration.

"Now it came to pass, about eight days after these sayings that He took Peter, John, and James and went up on the mountain to pray. As He prayed, the appearance of His face was altered, and His robe became white and glistening. And behold, two men talked with Him, who were Moses and Elijah, who appeared in glory and spoke of His decease which He was about to accomplish at Jerusalem. But Peter and those with him were heavy with sleep; and when they were fully awake, they saw His glory and the two men who stood with Him. Then it happened, as they were parting from Him, that Peter said to Jesus, 'Master, it is good for us to be here; and let us make three tabernacles: one for You, one for Moses, and one for Elijah'- not knowing what he said. While he was saying this, a cloud came and overshadowed them; and they were fearful as they entered the cloud. And a voice came out of the cloud, saying, 'This is My beloved Son. Hear Him!' when the voice had ceased, Jesus was found alone. But they kept quiet, and told no one in those days any of the things they had seen." Luke 9: 28-36 (NKJV)

The Father voices His pleasure in His Son, and you see the Father's Glory and the manifest presence of God. When you live in obedience to Jesus, and you have the pleasure of the Father in your life and ministry, you will see the manifestation of God's Glory. The anointing of Jesus in your life and ministry testifies to whom you are in the earth. But the Glory of God in your life and ministry testifies as to whom you are in the heavens with Jesus.

"Many will say to Me in that day, 'Lord, Lord, have we not prophesied in Your name, cast out demons in Your name, and done many wonders in Your name?' And then I will declare to them, 'I never knew you; depart from Me, you who practice lawlessness!'" Matthew 7:22-23 (NKJV)

Jesus says that many will come to Him in that day, saying that they have prophesied in His name, cast out devils in His name, and in His name have done many wonderful works. But instead, Jesus will say to them to depart from Him because of their iniquities.

These were people who had the anointing of Jesus and ministered out of their ministry identity. When Jesus said, "Depart from Me," this was what a Master Rabbi would have said to a junior rabbi, a student, or a disciple. In other words, the person failed the final test, and they were dismissed from the rabbi and the teacher.

> **"Then Jesus said to those Jews who believed Him, 'If you abide in My word, you are My disciples indeed. And you shall know the truth, and the truth shall make you free.' They answered Him, 'We are Abram's descendants, and have never been in bondage to anyone. How can You say, 'You will be made free?' Jesus answered them, 'Most assuredly, I say to you, whoever commits a sin is a slave of sin. And a slave does not abide in the house forever, but a son abides forever. Therefore, if the Son makes you free, you shall be free indeed.'" John 8:31-36 (NKJV)**

Jesus said a person could be a son, or a person could be a servant. A servant is not always in the house, but a son is there forever. Whoever the SON sets free is free in reality.

The Greek word for *free* is the word, *exempt*. In other words, Jesus said that If you continue in My Word, abide in Me, then you are My disciples in reality, and the truth will make you free or exempt from sin. You will not participate in it because God's Word is strong within you.

If you will abide in My Word, you remain in My Word and stay in MY Word in the Greek. It means that you persist in an activity or process so that you will move forward and grow in My Word. You become My disciple in reality.

In Greek, this passage means a servant does not continue to persist, but a son continues to the point of freedom and liberty.

> **"For as many as are led by the Spirit of God, these are the sons of God." Romans 8:14 (NKJV)**

Those who the Spirit of God leads are the mature sons of God.

> **"For to this you were called, because Christ also suffered for us, leaving us an example, that you should follow His steps:"**
> **1 Peter 2:21 (NKJV)**

We need to follow the example of Jesus.

> **"And Jesus came and spoke to them, saying, 'All authority has been given to Me in heaven and on earth. Go therefore and make disciples of all nations, baptizing them in the name of the Father and of the Son and of the Holy Spirit, teaching them to observe all things that I have commanded you; and lo, I am with you always,**

even to the end of the age.' Amen." Matthew 28: 18-20 (NKJV)

We need to make disciples and teach the nations. A real Son comes to think like Jesus, talk like Jesus, act like Jesus, and have a Jesus life. In some way, we need a Jesus ministry! It is time to walk in the reality of Jesus and the revelation of the Father.

Another key to knowing this Lord of Glory to desire the revelation that He is YOUR father, Abba God, and YOU are His son or daughter! He is YOUR Daddy!

CHAPTER 3:

The Revelation of the Father, Part 2

The Father taught Jesus to minister out of His identity as a Son. The first ministry of Jesus was to the Father Himself. Jesus was led to receive the Spirit of the Father.

> "When all the people were baptized, it came to pass that Jesus also was baptized; and while He prayed, the heaven was opened. And the Holy Spirit descended in bodily form like a dove upon him, and a voice came from heaven which said, 'You are My beloved Son; in You I am well pleased.'" Luke 3:21-23 (NKJV)

The Father filled Jesus with the Spirit.

"Then Jesus being filled with the Holy Spirit..."
Luke 4:1 (NKJV)

Jesus chose to be led by the Spirit of the Father.

"Then Jesus, being filled with the Holy Spirit, returned from the Jordan and was led by the Spirit into the wilderness," Luke 4:1 (NKJV)

Jesus obeyed the Word of the Father.

"And Jesus, answering, spoke to the lawyers and Pharisees, saying, 'Is it lawful to heal on the Sabbath?' But they kept silent. And He took him and healed him and let him go. Then He answered them, saying, 'Which of you, having a donkey or an ox that has fallen into a pit, will not immediately pull him out on the Sabbath day?' And they could not answer Him regarding these things." Luke 14: 1-6 (NKJV)

Jesus returned in the power of the Spirit.

"Then Jesus returned in the power of the Spirit to Galilee, and news of Him went out through all the surrounding region." Luke 4:14 (NKJV)

The Father assigned angels to the life and ministry of Jesus

"...and the angels ministered to Him." Mark 1:13 (NKJV)

"For it is written: 'He shall give His angels charge over you, To keep you,'" Luke 4:10 (NKJV)

Jesus would wake up before daylight and spend time with the Father.

"Now in the morning, having risen a long while before daylight, He went out and departed to a solitary place; and there He prayed." Mark 1: 35 (NKJV)

Jesus would pray to the Father as He went through the day.

"Now it came to pass, as He was praying in a certain place, when He ceased, that one of His disciples said to Him, 'Lord, teach us to pray, as John taught his disciples." Luke 11:1 (NKJV)

There were times when Jesus would spend part of the night or all night talking to the Father.

"Now it came to pass in those days that He went out to the mountain to pray, and continued all night in prayer to God." Luke 6:12 (NKJV)

The second ministry of the Lord Jesus was to HIMSELF. How did He do this? The apostle Paul explained it this way.

"So now, brethren, I commend you to God and to the word of His grace, which is able to build you up and give you an inheritance among all those who are sanctified." Acts 20:32 (NKJV)

Jesus studied the written word of God, and then this is what He did. Christ built His Spirit by thinking, speaking, and doing the Word of the Father in the old covenant. Then Jesus did four things.

1. Jesus used His faith in His flesh to obey the Word of the Father.

2. Jesus used His faith to get His prayers answered by the Father.

3. Jesus used His faith to minister in the gifts of the HOLY SPIRIT.

4. Jesus used His faith to manifest the Father's Glory!

The Lord Jesus was able to do these things because He received the revelations of the Father.

"Then Jesus answered and said to them, 'Most assuredly, I say to you, the Son can do nothing of Himself, but what He sees the Father do; for whatever He does, the Son also does in like manner. For the Father loves the Son, and shows him all things that He himself does; and He will show Him greater works than these, that you may marvel.'" John 5:19-20 (NKJV)

"Then Jesus said to them, 'When you lift up the Son of Man, then you will know that I am He, and that I do nothing of Myself; but as My

Father taught Me, I speak these things.'" John 8:28 (NKJV)

"But I have a greater witness than John's; for the works which the Father has given Me to finish---the very works that I do---bear witness of Me, that the Father has sent Me." John 5:36 (NKJV)

"But Jesus answered them, 'My Father has been working until now, and I have been working.'" John 5:17 (NKJV)

"Believe Me that I am in the Father and the Father in Me, or else believe Me for the sake of the works themselves." John 14:11 (NKJV)

The Lord Jesus lived His life hearing the voice of the Father and receiving visions by the Spirit of the Father so that He would know what to say and do in His life and ministry. The Lord Jesus lived his life in a dialogue with the Father. He said, "Follow Me," so His intention is that *you* live your life in a dialogue with the Father too. *You* need to build your spirit up by the written word of God. *You* need to hear the voice of the Father to receive visions from the Spirit of the Father. *You* need to live the kind of life Jesus did, and *you* need to do His works.

The third ministry of the Lord Jesus was to the people.

"And Jesus went about all of Galilee, teaching in their synagogues, preaching the gospel of the kingdom, and healing all kinds of sickness

and all kinds of disease among the people. Then His fame went throughout Syria; and they brought to him all sick people who were afflicted with various diseases and torments, and those who were demon-possessed, epileptics, and paralytics; and He healed them." Matthew 4:23-24 (NKJV)

Jesus preached the good news concerning the Kingdom of God. He taught in the synagogues, and He healed every kind of sickness and every kind of disease among the people. Jesus healed pain. Jesus cast out devils. Jesus healed people of mental illnesses, and He healed people of paralysis. It was the Father who taught Jesus how to heal every sickness and disease. And, by the Spirit of the Father, Jesus taught his disciples how to bring divine healing.

"Heal the sick, cleanse the lepers, raise the dead, cast out demons. Freely you have received, freely give." Matthew 10:8 (NKJV)

Just like the Father taught Jesus, Jesus can teach *you* by the Spirit of the Father to bring salvation, healing, deliverance, and freedom to people so that *you* can participate in the harvest of souls and make disciples of Christ.

Another key to knowing this Lord of Glory is to learn to minister to the Father, the Son, and His people, just as Jesus did!

CHAPTER 4:

How to Know the FATHER OF GLORY

"I and My Father are one." John10:30 (NKJV)

"...He who has seen Me has seen the Father; so how can you say, 'Show us the Father'? Do you not believe that I am in the Father, and the Father in Me? The words that I speak to you I do not speak on my own authority; but the Father who dwells in Me does the works." John 14: 9-10 (NKJV)

"If you had known Me, you would have known My Father also; and from now on you know Him and have seen Him." John 14:7 (NKJV)

Jesus clarifies that He did not speak on His own authority, but whatever He spoke, it was the words given to Him by the Father. Jesus said it was the Father who works through Him.

> "... 'Most assuredly, I say to you, the Son can do nothing of Himself, but what He sees the Father do; for whatever He does, the Son also does in like manner.'" John 5:19 (NKJV)

It is very clear from the Word of God that the purpose of Jesus was to reveal the person of the Father. Jesus wanted to show both the character and the ability of the Father.

> "And behold, a leper came and worshiped him, saying, 'Lord, if You are willing, You can make me clean.' Then Jesus put out his hand and touched him, saying, 'I am willing; be cleansed.' Immediately his leprosy was cleansed."
> Matthew 8: 2-3 (NKJV)

When Jesus meets this leper, the leper says, "If You are willing." Jesus responds and reveals the FATHER by saying, "I do want to cleanse you with all of MY heart." After that, Jesus touches the leper, and immediately his leprosy is cleansed. This is an example where it is made clear that it is the Father's heart to bring spiritual, mental, emotional, and physical healing to the hurting. Everywhere Jesus went, HE revealed the HEART and the WILL of the FATHER by removing sickness and healing disease.

> "A woman of Samaria came to draw water. Jesus said to her, 'Give Me a drink.' For His disciples had gone away into the city to buy

food. Then the woman of Samaria said to Him, 'How is it that You, being a Jew, ask a drink from me, a Samaritan woman?' For Jew have no dealings with Samaritans. Jesus answered and said to her, 'If you knew the gift of God, and who it is who says to you, 'Give Me a drink,' you would have asked Him, and He would have given you living water.' The woman said to him, 'Sir, you have nothing to draw with, and the well is deep. Where then do you get that living water? Are You greater than our father Jacob, who gave us the well and drank from it himself, as well as his sons and livestock?' Jesus answered and said to her, 'Whoever drinks of this water will thirst again, but whoever drinks of the water that I shall give him will never thirst.' John 4:7-14 (NKJV)

In John, chapter 4, Jesus interacts with a woman and a well. Jesus treated the woman with dignity and respect, and yet, at the same time, He brought conviction to her heart. He told her the truth about her life by revelation, and He loved her into repentance, salvation, and deliverance!

Jesus shows us that the Father treats people with dignity and respect even though He one hundred percent disagrees with their behavior or way of life. He makes it known to us that the Father was not out to condemn but was wanting to convince this woman to change her way of life. In both examples, Jesus shows that the Father does not reject but loves and accepts, changes, and transforms a person by His mercy and His grace!

"Then the scribes and Pharisees brought to him a woman caught in adultery. And when they had set her in their midst, they said to Him, 'Teacher, this woman was caught in adultery, in the very act.'" John 8: 3-4 (NKJV)

"So when they continued asking Him, He raised himself up and said to them, 'He who is without sin among you, let him throw a stone at her first.'" John 8:7 NKJV)

"...And Jesus said to her, 'Neither do I condemn you; go and sin no more.'" John 8:11 (NKJV)

Notice the woman who was caught in adultery clearly violated the Father's commandment, and yet, the Father works through Jesus to keep her from being judged and stoned. He showed her mercy and grace and then instructed her to go and "sin no more."

If the woman was caught in adultery, why didn't the men bring a man? The Father revealed to Jesus that the men were the ones who committed adultery with the woman. And yet, the Father was unwilling to expose the men who had exposed the woman and wanted to cause her to be stoned, as well as hurt Jesus. The compassion and kindness of the Father was clearly seen by the judgment of God that extended mercy and grace to save the woman's life!

"But woe to you, scribes and Pharisees, hypocrites! For you shut up the kingdom of heaven against men; for you neither go in

yourselves, nor do you allow those who are entering to go in." Matthew 23:13 (NKJV)

"Then Jesus went into the temple of God and drove out all those who bought and sold in the temple, and overturned the tables of the money changers and the seats of those who sold doves." Matthew 21: 12 (NKJV)

These are the only times you see Jesus showing you the anger of the Father. He confronted the Pharisees for their hypocrisy in Matthew, chapter 23, and He drove out the ministers in the temple who were merchandising in the name of the Lord God, in Matthew, chapter 21.

The FATHER gave HIS SON to die for those HE cared about to bring many sons and daughters into Glory! Jesus gave the Father His dream, which was to bring to God many sons and daughters. YOU are the Father's dream. YOU are the one the Father yearns for and longs for. YOU are the one that the Father honors and respects. YOU are the one that the Father cherishes and treasures!

Knowing that the Father and Jesus are ONE is an important key to the Glory!

CHAPTER 5:

The Glory and Divine Guidance

"And it shall come to pass afterward that I will pour out My Spirit on all flesh; Your sons and your daughters shall prophesy, Your old men shall dream dreams, Your young men shall see visions." Joel 2: 28 (NKJV)

When I was pastoring, an older woman was praying very intensely that she really wanted to be ready to meet Jesus when she passed away. One night, the Spirit and the Glory of God came upon her, and she had a dream. In the dream, she was in a church, and the Lord Jesus walked up to her, and this is what He said: *"What I want from you are three things. I want the same three things from everyone. First, bring Me the fruit of repentance. Second, practice righteousness every day. Third, develop intimacy with Me."*

Then the Lord Jesus demanded a response from this woman, and this is the question that He asked, "Will you do this?" At this point, the woman replied "Yes," and Jesus put His hand on her as the great high priest and prayed to the Father for her.

After that, she saw Jesus walk away, smile at someone else, and then say the same thing to that person that He just said to her. Then the dream or vision ended. It was an outpouring of the Holy Spirit, the Spirit of God's Glory, that gave her the dream or the vision. Jesus said that the Holy Spirit, the Spirit of God's Glory, would testify about Jesus. Was this a biblical vision?

"Therefore, bear fruits worthy of repentance," Matthew 3:8 (NKJV)

Here the prophet John tells the people who came to him to bring forth fruit in keeping with repentance. The Greek word *repent* means to change your mind or make a different decision. The Hebrew word *repent* means to actually physically turn around. The Old Testament was primarily written in Hebrew, while the New Testament was written in Greek. When you put the meanings of the two words together, a person hears the Word of God, changes his mind, conforms, yields to, and then obeys the Word of God. That is repentance.

Repentance is an act of yielding to, conforming to, and actually obeying what God's Word says. When the Glory of God comes into your life, the Spirit of the Lord calls you into deeper and deeper repentance to make you more and more like Jesus.

"Little children, let no one deceive you. He who practices righteousness is righteous, just as He is righteous." 1 John 3:7 (NKJV)

When the Glory of God comes, you are instructed by the Lord Jesus to practice righteousness.

"For the Lord is righteous, He loves righteousness; His countenance beholds the upright." Psalm 11:7 (NKJV)

"Because it is written, 'Be holy, for I am holy.'"1 Peter 1: 16 (NKJV)

This is a true word from the Lord.

When the Spirit of God's Glory is poured out, you will get the revelation of what God's will is for your private life.

"If you are reproached for the name of Christ, blessed are you, for the Spirit of Glory and of God rests upon you. On their part He is blasphemed, but on your part, He is glorified." 1 Peter 4: 14 (NKJV)

The Holy Spirit of God is the Spirit of Glory.

"Which none of the rulers of this age knew; for had they known, they would not have crucified the Lord of glory." 1 Corinthians 2:8 (NKJV)

Jesus is called the Lord of Glory.

"that the God of our Lord Jesus Christ, the Father of glory, may give to you the spirit of wisdom and revelation in the knowledge of Him," Ephesians 1:17 (NKJV)

God is called the Father of Glory.

"that I may know Him and the power of His resurrection, and the fellowship of His sufferings, being conformed to his death," Philippians 3:10 (NKJV)

This is a direct reference to having an intimate relationship with the Lord Jesus. Over and over again, the Word of God talks about the importance of *knowing* the Lord.

"Now by this we know that we know Him, if we keep His commandments." 1 John 2:3 (NKJV)

The biggest reason you and I need to have the Glory of God in our lives is that it is a key to knowing Jesus intimately. Personal guidance is the result of knowing God by the presence of His Glory through Jesus!

CHAPTER 6:

The Glory and Pleasing the Father

During the early 1900s, the Azusa Street revival took place in Los Angeles, California. During that time, people saw the fire of God shoot up fifty feet into the sky and then be joined by a fire of God that came down from the Heavens. In addition to that, there was a physical Glory Cloud inside the building that was so thick that children played hide-and-seek within it.

Because of the Glory, there were all kinds of miracles that were experienced, just as those described in God's Word.

> "to another the working of miracles, to another prophecy, to another discerning of spirits, to another different kinds of tongues, to another

the interpretation of tongues."
1 Corinthians 12:10 (NKJV)

There were great miracles:

"And Stephen, full of faith and power, did great wonders and signs among the people." Acts 6:8 (NKJV)

There were amazing miracles.

"... 'Silver or gold I do not have, but what I do have I give you. In the name of Jesus Christ of Nazareth, walk.'" Acts 3: 6 (NIV)

Peter healed the lame beggar in the name of Jesus, proclaimed with courage the resurrection of Jesus Christ, was jailed and released, and then returned to the believers, where after prayer,

"... the place where they were meeting was shaken. And they were all filled with the Holy Spirit and spoke the word of God boldly." Acts 4: 31 (NIV)

And, there were extraordinary miracles:

"God did extraordinary miracles through Paul, so that even handkerchiefs and aprons that had touched him were taken to the sick, and their illnesses were cured and the evil spirits left them." Acts 19: 11 (NIV)

When the GLORY is present, the Spirit of prophecy can also manifest. Here is one such prophecy that came out of the Glory of God during the Azusa Street revival.

"It shall come to pass in the latter days of the great Pentecostal revival that three things will occur. The people will praise a GOD they no longer pray to. They will emphasize power instead of righteousness. They will focus on the gifts of the SPIRIT rather than the LORDSHIP of JESUS CHRIST."

I love the anointing of the Holy Spirit, but when a person focuses on the anointing only, praise, power, and the gifts of the Spirit will be emphasized. The Glory of God teaches you to focus on prayer and then praise. The Glory of God teaches you to focus on righteousness and then the power of the Spirit. The GLORY OF GOD teaches you to focus on the LORDSHIP of JESUS CHRIST and then His precious gifts. The GLORY OF GOD brings you into DIVINE ORDER so that you may PLEASE the FATHER IN THE SPIRIT OF JESUS CHRIST.

"Therefore, I exhort first of all that supplications, prayers, intercessions, and giving of thanks be made for all men," 1 Timothy 2:1 (NKJV)

Timothy was encouraged by the Holy Spirit to begin with prayers, supplications, and intercessions, and then the giving of thanks. In divine order, according to the scriptures, things begin with prayers, supplications, and intercessions. Then we begin to thank and give praise to the Father. Think about how many services actually begin with praise and worship rather than intense prayer. Think about how people love to attend praise and worship services but fail to attend prayer meetings.

> **"Finally, then, brethren, we urge and exhort in the Lord Jesus that you should abound more and more, just as you received from us how you ought to walk and to please God;"**
> **1 Thessalonians 4: 1 (NKJV)**

When you pray, praise, worship, and obey the Word of God, you are pleasing to the Father. When you and I emphasize righteousness, and that becomes our way of life in Jesus Christ, we please the Father.

> **"that you may walk worthy of the Lord, fully pleasing Him, being fruitful in every good work and increasing in the knowledge of God;"**
> **Colossians 1: 10 (NKJV)**

We are commanded to walk worthy of the Lord and please Him in every way. As a result of that, He will make us fruitful in every work, and we will increase in the intimate knowledge of God. If we will please the Lord and live a righteous, holy life, we will see more of the power of the Spirit and become more fruitful in the name of Jesus.

> **"Then He said to them all, 'If anyone desires to come after Me, let him deny himself, and take up his cross daily, and follow Me.'" Luke 9: 23 (NKJV)**

If you can make it your purpose to follow after Jesus, to deny the self-life, to take up your cross, and to obey the teachings of Jesus, then you will move in the gifts of the Spirit and the Glory of God under the LORDSHIP of the CHRIST. This will bring joy to Jesus and gladness to the heart of the Father.

A key to having the Glory of God in your life is to make a commitment to the Lord Jesus and to be consistent in prayer, both in agreement with the WORD and in the PERSON of the HOLY SPIRIT!

CHAPTER 7:

The Friendship of the Holy Spirit

"The grace of the Lord Jesus Christ, and the love of God, and the communion of the Holy Spirit be with you all. Amen."
2 Corinthians 13:14 (NKJV)

The Greek word for *communion* is spelled *koinonia*. This word means you can have the FELLOWSHIP of the Holy Spirit, and you can have the FRIENDSHIP of the Holy Spirit. You can have the COMPANIONSHIP of the Holy Spirit, and you can have INTIMACY with the Holy Spirit. You can also have the PARTNERSHIP of the Holy Spirit. This Greek word also means RESPONSIBILITY. This means the Holy Spirit wants to be responsible for you. But you must also respond to the Holy Spirit for Him to work in you, both to will and to do God's pleasure.

> "that which we have seen and heard we declare to you, that you also may have fellowship with us; and truly our fellowship is with the Father and with His Son Jesus Christ."
> 1 John 1:3 (NKJV)

Our fellowship is with the Father and His Son, Jesus, but you can also have a relationship with the Holy Spirit. You can have a closeness with the Holy Spirit. Your heart can be attached to the Holy Spirit, and you may be able to sense, feel, or hear the Holy Spirit.

> "And the angel answered and said to her, 'The Holy Spirit will come upon you, and the power of the Highest will overshadow you; therefore, also, that Holy One who is to be born will be called the Son of God.'" Luke 1:35 (NKJV)

The Holy Spirit conceived the Lord Jesus in the virgin Mary by the Father.

> "Jesus answered, 'Most assuredly, I say to you, unless one is born of water and the Spirit, he cannot enter the kingdom of God. That which is born of the flesh is flesh, and that which is born of the spirit is spirit. Do not marvel that I said to you, 'You must be born again. The wind blows where it wishes, and you hear the sound of it, but cannot tell where it comes from and where it goes. So is everyone who is born of the Spirit.'" John 3: 5-8 (NKJV)

You have been born again by the Holy Spirit because of Jesus and the Father.

> "When He had been baptized, Jesus came up immediately from the water; and behold, the heavens opened to Him, and He saw the Spirit of God descending like a dove and alighting upon Him." Matthew 3: 16 (NKJV)

Jesus was filled with the Holy Spirit when He was baptized by John.

> "And they were all filled with the Holy Spirit and began to speak with other tongues, as the Spirit gave them utterance." Acts 2:4 (NKJV)

Because of Jesus, your heavenly Father has filled you with the Holy Spirit.

> "Then Jesus, being filled with the Holy Spirit, returned from the Jordan and was led by the Spirit into the wilderness," Luke 4:1 (NKJV)

Jesus was led by the Spirit.

> "For as many as are led by the Spirit of God, these are the sons of God." Romans 8:14 (NKJV)

Because of Jesus you are to be led by the Spirit.

> "The Spirit of the Lord is upon Me, because he has anointed Me to preach the gospel to the poor; He has sent Me to heal the

brokenhearted, to proclaim liberty to the captives and recovery of sight to the blind, to set at liberty those who are oppressed;" Luke 4:18 (NKJV)

Jesus was empowered by the Spirit to heal the sick, to expel demons, to raise the dead to life, and to do miracles.

"But you shall receive power when the Holy Spirit has come upon you; and you shall be witnesses to Me in Jerusalem, and in all Judea and Samaria, and to the end of the earth." Acts 1:8 (NKJV)

You have received power since the Holy Spirit has come upon you to do the same works that Jesus has done. The Lord Jesus had the fellowship, the friendship, the communion, the partnership, and the intimacy of the Spirit. HE was able to fulfill the will of Father. Let us follow in the steps of Jesus and develop such a relationship with the Holy Spirit that we too can have a holy life and do holy works in the name of Jesus!

The key to fulfilling the will of the Father is to develop fellowship, friendship, communion, partnership, and intimacy with the Holy Spirit!

CHAPTER 8:

How to Increase in the Glory of God

"But we all, with unveiled face, beholding as in a mirror the glory of the Lord, are being transformed into the same image from glory to glory, just as by the Spirit of the Lord." 2 Corinthians 3:18 (NKJV)

How do we grow in the Glory of God? Here the Word tells us that we see the Glory of God as we look into a mirror with an uncovered face, and we are changed from glory to glory by the Spirit of the Lord.

"The Lord is my shepherd; I shall not want. He makes me to lie down in green pastures; He leads me beside the still waters. He restores my soul; He leads me in the paths of righteousness for His name's sake.

Yea, though I walk through the valley of the shadow of death, I will fear no evil; for You are with me; Your rod and Your staff, they comfort me.

You prepare a table before me in the presence of my enemies; You anoint my head with oil; My cup runs over. Surely goodness and mercy shall follow me all the days of my life; and I will dwell in the house of the Lord forever." Psalm 23 (NKJV)

The prophet in this Hebrew song talks about the presence of God and the process that one walks through to grow in the Glory of the Lord and maturity in Jesus.

Sometimes we wonder about the process. Why do things nearly always take longer than we want them to?

"But as we were allowed of God to be put in trust with the gospel, even so we speak; not as pleasing men, but God, which trieth our hearts." 1 Thessalonians 2:4 (KJV)

The word *allowed* in the original language is the Greek word, *dokimazo*. It means to test, examine, inspect, scrutinize, or determine the quality or sincerity of a thing. If the object or the person being tested passes the test, it is considered to be genuine or sincere.

This Greek word was used to determine the difference between counterfeit and genuine coinage. It was earlier used to test metals. The metal was put into a fire to remove its impurities. There were three tests for the metals: mild, moderate, and severe. If the metal passed the third test, it was considered to be pure. The metal was tested because if it had any unseen impurities, it would break, fracture, or malfunction in some way.

The reason things do not happen as quickly as we would like is that God is trying us. He permits us to have one trial after the other to test our ability to stand and do HIS will even when we are under pressure. He allows us to go through a purifying process because what HE wants us to BECOME is more important to HIM than what HE is calling us to DO. He permits the cleansing process so we can BE and DO HIS good pleasure!

If we submit to God's holy process, regardless of how long it takes, we will see more results and greater results than ever! The process helps us to develop our faith, obedience, and patience, so we become more like Jesus--- more effective, more productive, and more powerful! As we obey the Word of God by faith and patience, we are promoted by JESUS! We are matured into the glorious image of Jesus Christ and conformed to His likeness!

> **"For whom He foreknew, He also predestined to be conformed to the image of His Son, that He might be the firstborn among many brethren." Romans 8:29 (NKJV)**

God predestined **you** to be conformed to the image of His Son, Jesus Christ.

> **"As for me, I will see Your face in righteousness; I shall be satisfied when I awake in Your likeness." Psalm 17: 15 (NKJV)**

The prophet says that he will look at the Lord's righteousness, and he shall be satisfied when he awakens in His likeness. Make *me* awaken in Your likeness! Make it so, oh God, by Your glorious presence in the name of Jesus!

> *The key to increasing in the Glory of God is obedience to the Word of God so that your faith is developed through patience and His presence!*

CHAPTER 9:

The Supply of the Holy Spirit

"For I know that this shall turn to my salvation through your prayer, and the supply of the Spirit of Jesus Christ," Philippians 1:19 (KJV)

The word *supply* here is the Greek word *epichore-geo*. It means that something is done on behalf of another person. The story behind the word is that of a drama company that practiced for a performance but then ran out of money before the performance could be given. A wealthy donor gave them all the money that was needed so that they could actually give a public performance.

Here, Paul was saying that through *your* prayers and intercessions, the Holy Spirit will give *him* everything that he needs. This means that prayer and intercession cause a supernatural supply of the Spirit--- more than enough abundance! In other words, the Holy Spirit will give you the spiritual, mental, emotional, physical, or financial assistance you need when you pray for others. He will give you *over and above* what is required so that you have all the resources necessary to fulfill your God-given calling and assignment!

The Holy Spirit is the Spirit of Glory, and in the Glory of God, there is a supernatural supply for you or another because of the sacrifice, death, and resurrection of the Lord Jesus Christ!

Here is a manifestation of God's Glory in the area of healing. I was doing a meeting in Decatur, Illinois, at an Assembly of God church. A man who had been blind in one eye for thirty years instantly began to see because of the manifest presence of Jesus. A supernatural supply of Glory caused a blind eye to see.

Here is a manifestation of God's Glory in the area of finance. Because of the supernatural presence of God, a man was given a raise of over three thousand dollars a month!

If you will believe the Word of God and receive our prayer of faith and intercession, there can be a supply of the Spirit that will bring healing and/or additional finances to you in the name of Jesus!

The key to the supernatural supply of the Holy Spirit is through prayer and intercession for others!

CHAPTER 10:

Walk in the Spirit and the Glory

"For as many as are led by the Spirit of God, they are the sons of God." Romans 8:14 (KJV)

In the Greek language, this sentence structure is different than in English. It would read in the Greek this way: *For as many as by the Holy Spirit are being led, they are the sons of God.* In other words, a believer follows the person of the Holy Spirit. In Greek, the word for *led* is the word *ago,* which means to lead.

The history of the word references when an owner took an animal and put a rope around its neck to lead that animal where he wanted it to go. That animal with the rope around its neck was in submission to the owner.

"Now the Lord is the Spirit; and where the Spirit of the Lord is, there is liberty." 2 Corinthians 3:17 (NKJV)

The child of God must be in submission to the Spirit of Jesus and allow himself to be led by the Lord. The Bible says that the Lord is the Holy Spirit and that the Holy Spirit is the Lord.

The word, *ago,* is connected to the word *agon,* which means agony. The reference for this word means "a struggle of the human will." The Holy Spirit may struggle with a man to get that man to surrender so he will do the Word and walk in the way of God. This means that sometimes a person may feel as if they are in agony as they allow themselves to be led by the Holy Spirit. A child of God must be like Jesus and say, "HOLY FATHER, not my will, but YOUR WILL be done." It is a matter of yielding to the Holy Spirit.

When a person is driving and sees a yield sign, it means he should let the other person go first. When a believer in Jesus yields to the Holy Spirit, he puts the Word of God and Jesus first. He obeys the voice and the leadership of the Holy Spirit!

When a person yields to the Spirit of Christ, it is the result of saying yes to God. Yielding is the absence of resistance. It is very easy for us to resist Holy Spirit. A person must be willing to say *no* to himself, *yes* to Jesus, and yield to the Holy Spirit so that God's will is done.

"I say then: Walk in the Spirit, and you shall not fulfill the lust of the flesh." Galatians 5: 16 (NKJV)

To walk after and in the Holy Spirit is to walk in the GLORY! Remember the SPIRIT of the LORD is the SPIRIT of GOD'S's GLORY.

"If you are reproached for the name of Christ, blessed are you, for the Spirit of glory and of God rests upon you. On their part He is blasphemed, but on your part, He is glorified." 1 Peter 4: 14 (NKJV)

You are blessed when the SPIRIT of GLORY and of GOD rests upon you! When a person walks after the SPIRIT, he walks into the GLORY, becoming more like JESUS CHRIST!

The key to spiritual maturity is walking after the Holy Spirit and living in the Glory by loving and obeying Jesus!

CHAPTER 11:

How to find your Marriage Partner by the Glory

"Cause me to hear your lovingkindness in the morning, for in You do I trust; Cause me to know the way in which I should walk, for I lift my soul to You." Psalm 143:8 (NKJV)

"For as many as are led by the Spirit of God, they are the sons of God." Romans 8:14 (KJV)

The Holy Spirit is the Spirit of Glory. So as many as are led by the Glory of God are the sons of God. The Spirit and the Glory of God can lead you to find your mate.

"Search from the book of the Lord, and read: Not one of these shall fail; Not one shall lack her mate. For My mouth has commanded it,

and His Spirit has gathered them." Isaiah 34:16 (NKJV)

The prophet Isaiah gives this instruction. Find the book of the Lord and read it. Those who do so shall not fail. They shall find their mate, for the mouth of God has commanded it, and the Spirit of the Lord will gather them together.

I know a man who when he was twenty-two years of age spent time in the Word of God and was walking in the Holy Spirit. This young man could not find a woman that he wanted to marry in any of the churches that he attended, and at the time, he himself was a youth pastor. Though he had been in college and had great friends, he still could not find anyone that fit his life and his calling.

One Sunday, this young man was fasting and praying, and a visiting minister was coming to the church. A woman and her mother felt led by the Spirit of God to come from another state to this meeting. Before this woman got to the meeting, she heard a voice that said, "You are getting ready to meet someone."

This woman walked up to the young pastor at the meeting and started a conversation. At the end of the service, the Spirit of God said to the young man, "This woman is going to be your wife".

He said nothing to the young woman at that time, but he did get her name and address. The young woman and her mother went home, but this young woman felt a connection to this man. She asked her mother to pray about the young man, and the Spirit of God told her mother that this young man would be her daughter's husband.

Later the Holy Spirit spoke to the young woman and gave her the same message. This young man and the young woman began to see each other, and the Lord used another pastor to counsel them. He confirmed that they were to get married and told them what they needed to do for the next fifteen years. They followed the instructions of God. They have now been married for over forty years and have served Jesus in ministry together for all of those years.

There have been so many different occasions in which I have witnessed the Glory of God bring compatible people together! It is such a supernatural event by the goodness of God. Perhaps you or someone you care about are just having difficulty finding a mate. Allow me to pray this prayer and release the Glory of God into your life.

Holy Father, I send the presence of your Glory right now to this one who needs a mate! Let the Spirit of God move supernaturally to bring the two that are destined in Your will to meet and be together! Holy FATHER, release your wonderful angels right now, according to Your Word, so that each one finds his/her mate in Jesus's name!

The key to walking in the Glory is to hear and obey the Word of the Lord!

CHAPTER 12:

Marriage in the Glory of God

There had been a move of God in the local community where the Lord Jesus Christ was touching a number of young people. One evening after a meeting, I was at a restaurant. I looked at a man, and I heard a voice say, "Go home to your wife." It was 11 o'clock P.M. I did not know it at the time, but this man had promised his wife that he would be home at eleven, but he did not leave and get home according to the time that he had promised her.

Later, I had the blessing of being in the home of this young man and his wife. He had been a drug user and a drug dealer who had been gloriously saved and delivered by Jesus. While I was sitting there, visiting with him and his wife, the Glory presence of God came into the living room, and I was suddenly given revelation knowledge that his wife was afraid of losing her husband to Jesus, just like she had lost him to drugs. When

I asked her if this was true, she confirmed it. The voice of the Lord told me that they needed to start praying together. I encouraged them to do so.

Later, when I was back home, it was reported to me that this couple were now getting along much better. By praying together, they were communicating and sharing their thoughts and feelings with each other. They ended up spending more time together, which brought them closer to one another by the Glory presence of the Lord!

When the Glory of God comes, revelation knowledge flows.

"Then the Lord said to Samuel: 'Behold, I will do something in Israel at which both ears of everyone who hears it will tingle. In that day I will perform against Eli all that I have spoken concerning his house, from beginning to end." 1 Samuel 3: 11-12 (NKJV)

While serving the priest, Eli, the young boy, Samuel, was lying down near the Ark of the Covenant. The Lord came and began to speak, giving Samuel revelation knowledge. Remember, the Glory is the personal presence of the Lord in which HE begins to manifest HIMSELF to you. The boy, Samuel, began to know about the high priest, Eli, and what was going on in his family. As a result of the Glory of God, Samuel received prophetic insight and foresight.

The Holy Spirit can give knowledge, wisdom, and understanding to a couple so that their marriage can be better. For example, there are different kinds of marriages, and there are different roles that spouses play in a marriage. Sometimes, one spouse fulfills the role of a parent, and the other, the role of a child. In other relationships, each spouse plays the role of a child. Then, there are marriages that are adult to adult.

When the relationship is parent to child, one person is controlling, and the other person is controlled. The one who acts as the parent is basically saying "I'm OK" but to the child spouse, "You are not OK." This relationship will not work long-term. Unless relationships and emotions are healed and corrected, this couple will end in a divorce.

Sometimes each spouse may be chronologically an adult, but emotionally, each one makes decisions and behaves like a child. Unless each marriage partner is emotionally healed and learns how to behave according to his chronological age, this relationship will also fail and end in divorce. Because each spouse wants to have his own way, there is a lack of maturity and an inability or unwillingness to compromise or work together.

When one partner does not get his way, he is basically saying, "You're not OK and I'm not OK ". This person is saying, "I'm only OK when I get my way, and you're only OK when you give me my way".

This relationship will not work.

In the adult-to-adult relationship, each person is able to give and take and negotiate win-win situations so that they can be happy together. The attitude of each spouse toward the other is "You are OK, and I am OK".

"For the Lord God is a sun and shield; The Lord will give grace and glory; No good thing will He withhold from those who walk uprightly." Psalm 84:11 (NKJV)

In other words, when you walk in the light of God's Word, HE shines on you! HE releases HIS grace and HIS glory into your marriage so it can be filled with the wisdom and beauty of Jesus!

If we would only listen to the Holy Spirit and refrain from saying to our spouses what we want to in the flesh. When HE urges us to remain silent, and we do, things go so much more smoothly. Sometimes we think that being honest means we share everything we think and feel in the moment. Consider what would happen if you did that in your job or your career. You call up your boss or supervisor, and you say to him that you are not coming in today because you are just not feeling it. You probably will not have that job for long!

The best thing you can do sometimes is just "sit on yourself" and not say that thing to your spouse that you want to in your flesh nature. Sometimes you should ask the Father if it is even something that should be said at all. Once it is said, you cannot take it back, and it may do more harm than good.

Sometimes, when something does need to be communicated, you need to spend time first with Jesus. He will tell you when to say it, how to say it, how to control the tone of voice, the timing, and all those other little things that need to be considered in the Spirit of the Lord. When you follow the Spirit and the Glory of God, you will find the desired outcomes.

> "He who does not love does not know God, for God is love." 1 John 4:8 (NKJV)

> "Husbands, love your wives, just as Christ also loved the church and gave Himself for her, that He might sanctify and cleanse her with the washing of the water by the word, that He might present her to Himself a glorious church, not having spot or wrinkle or any such thing, but that she should be holy and without blemish." Ephesians 5: 25-27 (NKJV)

The Word of the Lord tells us that God's love is unconditional love. When Paul teaches husbands to love their wives, he uses the same Greek word, *agape*, for unconditional love. Paul was led by the Spirit and the Glory of God in this teaching. Paul does not use the word for sexual love, *eros.* Paul does not use the word for family love, *storge.* Paul does not use the word for friendship love, *philia.* Paul uses the word for unconditional love, *agape.*

Paul simply tells husbands to love their wives as Christ loves the church with His unconditional love. Unconditional love simply loves *without any conditions.*

> "Love suffers long and is kind; love does not envy; love does not parade itself, is not puffed up; does not behave rudely, does not seek its own, is not provoked, thinks no evil; does not

rejoice in iniquity, but rejoices in truth; bears
all things, believes all things, hopes all things,
endures all things. Love never fails..."
1 Corinthians 13: 4- 8 (NKJV)

The Glory of God is all that GOD is in His character and
in His ability! That means the Glory is the love of God!
When a husband loves his wife the way Jesus loves us,
he is loving his wife by the Glory of God Himself. Because this love is self-sacrificial, it makes it easy for his
wife to submit. Husbands, if you meet your wife's need
with the love and Glory of God, she will surrender and
follow your lead. The Glory of God in your love for her
releases the presence of the Lord, so that she will submit to you because she knows you have put her first,
just like Jesus puts you first!

"Wives, submit to your own husbands, as to the
Lord." Ephesians 5:22 (NKJV)

When a wife submits herself to her husband by the Spirit of God, it is a manifestation of the Lord's Glory! When
the two are submitted to Jesus, they have the power of
agreement and they can get their prayers answered by
the Father God!

"Again, I say to you that if two of you agree
on earth concerning anything they ask, it will
be done for them by My Father in heaven."
Matthew 18:19 (NKJV)

When a husband and wife agree, the Father of Glory releases His power and dramatic answers to prayer and

manifestations of the power of the Holy Spirit will be seen. The call of God is to have marriage in the Glory!

The key to having a marriage in the Glory is for both husband and wife to love each other unconditionally, as Christ loves His church!

CHAPTER 13:

Raising Children in the Glory Part 1

"The glory of the Lord shall be revealed. And all flesh shall see it together; For the mouth of the Lord has spoken." Isaiah 40:5 (NKJV)

"But Jesus said, 'Let the little children come to Me, and do not forbid them; for of such is the kingdom of heaven.'" Matthew 19:14 (NKJV)

"Therefore, whoever humbles himself as this little child is the greatest in the kingdom of heaven." Matthew 18:4 (NKJV)

Children are wonderful because of their faith and their innocence. Children are authentic, real, and genuine. There is true honesty in a child. I would love it if the Spirit of God, His Glory, would give me the faith, the genuineness, and the authenticity of a child before my heavenly Father.

When my wife and I got married, she was told by the physician that she could not have any children. My response to that was very simple. I said to her, "When I say that you are going to get pregnant, that is when it is going to happen."

> **"Jesus said to her, 'Did I not say to you that if you would believe you would see the glory of God?'" John 11:40 (NKJV)**

Jesus is speaking here to Lazarus's sister. She saw her brother raised from the dead! This tells me that when you have faith in the promises of God, it releases the Glory presence and the power of the Lord Jesus Christ!

My wife did get pregnant. About three months into the pregnancy, she began to bleed, and the doctor was very concerned that she had lost the baby. However, I remember sensing the anointing and the Glory of God, giving me the message that everything was going to be all right.

The Glory of God can give you supernatural rest!

> **"And He said, 'My Presence will go with you, and I will give you rest.'" Exodus 33:14 (NKJV)**

Here God speaks to the prophet Moses, and He gives him this word, "MY PRESENCE will go with you, and I will give you rest!"

When you find yourself in a crisis, you need the Glory of God to give you supernatural peace and rest. Moses was dependent upon God, and through his faith, he was given a supernatural peace and rest by the Glory of the Lord. He was able to become a successful leader and overcome all things. Whatever *you* are facing right now, the Glory presence of God can make *you* an overcomer too!

At first, the physician thought that the baby was dead in the womb, but when he checked my wife, he found that the baby was fine. When she delivered the child, the baby boy was completely healthy. JESUS is the resurrection, and HE is the life. All praise to Jesus and the Father!

When our son, Philip, was two years of age, he gave his heart to Jesus. From a very early age, he was taught the Word of God, and to pray, praise, and love Jesus. When he was eight years of age, he had a dream, and in the dream, he was called by God into the ministry. He saw himself preaching the good news about Jesus Christ. In this dream, he also saw an angel that told him that my wife and I would have the finances necessary to purchase a house. Within thirty days, that money was made available, and that house was purchased. It confirmed to us that Philip was genuinely called to be a minister of Jesus Christ.

Since that time, Philip and his wife have been in a number of countries preaching the gospel of Jesus and are currently ministering here in the United States. The Glory of God can do wonders for people regardless of how they were raised.

My wife and I know a woman who, when she was younger, was expelled from her home, and so, she was homeless. She was gloriously saved by Jesus one day and delivered from her addictions by the power and Glory of God! She was filled with the Holy Spirit and went on to walk with Jesus. She got her doctorate and has been successful in her life because of the grace and the Glory that is found in Christ Jesus!

The Word, the wisdom, the power, and the Glory of God can save a child or young person and deliver them fully in the name of Jesus. May I urge you not to depend upon the senior pastor, associate pastor, or the youth pastor to raise your child for Jesus! They have their part to play, but *you* must give your child the Word of God as often as possible on a weekly basis. Get your child filled with the Holy Spirit and show your child how to read and study the Bible. Fast, pray, and obey Jesus, and your children will follow your steps into the Glory of God!

The key to raising children in the Glory is to set the example for them by fasting, praying, and obeying the Word of God!

CHAPTER 14:

Raising Children in the Glory Part Two

"Fathers, don't exasperate your children by coming down hard on them. Take them by the hand and lead them in the way of the Master."
Ephesians 6:4 (MSG)

The word *exasperate* means to provoke your child to anger or to drive someone into a rage. In other words, because of the actions or reactions of the father (or the mother), the child becomes very angry, and then begins to rebel against them, and whatever it is they have been teaching. You can *know* what provokes your child to anger and rebellion, by what you have observed in the past, that has created those feelings within your child. You can also ask the Holy Spirit to show you what you need to know.

Do not discipline when you are angry. Remember that your words will shape your child's world. Emphasize the positive traits and characteristics of your child that you have observed to improve his personal esteem. Be truthful. Do not make up false attributes. They will see through your untruths. *All* children have positive traits. Some are harder to see and find than others. Ask the Lord to make you more aware of those little things that may have slipped past you. Encourage your child as much as you can. Build-up his personal confidence as much as you are able.

Just as you want the Lord to encourage, edify, and strengthen you, do so for your own sons and daughters. Just as you want the Lord to be gentle and kind when he corrects you, do so with your own children. Just as you do not want the Lord to be hard or harsh towards you, avoid those reactions with your own sons and daughters.

It is the Glory heart of God that encourages, comforts, edifies, and gives you confidence. The Glory love of God is not hard, harsh, or overbearing when correcting you but is gentle, kind, and good. Behave towards your own child or children as you would prefer your heavenly Father to do unto you.

If you put Jesus first in your own life, you increase the likelihood that your children will follow in your steps. In the very same way that you want to experience the person and the presence of the Father God in your life, you need to be there for your children. When you are there for your children with love and kindness, as well as correction, direction, teaching, and training, you can influence them to follow the Word of God and yield to the Spirit of Christ more fully.

Make family time a priority. Attend and participate as much as possible in the activities of your children. Let them know that they are special to you and that what they do matters to you. Read the Bible and pray together. Talk about the Word of God and attend meetings with each other. Let your children see you repent, exercise faith, and respond to the presence of the Lord in your life. Serve others with your children. Let them see the Glory of God manifested in serving others through the love of Jesus. Let your children see you share your faith with others.

> **"Train up a child in the way he should go,**
> **And when he is old he will not depart from it."**
> **Proverbs 22: 6 (NKJV)**

This scripture in Hebrew means *that the presence of the Lord shows you the child's natural and spiritual gifts to cultivate into maturity and become the keys to the child's success.* When he is old, he will not depart from that.

The best way to do this is to "walk the talk." Let your children see you follow Jesus. Ask Father God to give you discernment by the Holy Spirit so that you can identify, affirm, and validate the natural and spiritual gifts of your children. The Spirit of God will lead you to tell your child, "I believe in you and in the abilities that you've been given by Jesus!"

Usually, as fathers and mothers, we have a tendency to call our children "out" on their misbehaviors, but instead, we need to give them a higher standard and call them "up" into Jesus Christ. We need to give them a positive identity in Christ so that they will know how to behave as Godly persons through the Holy Spirit.

Show your children how much you love your spouse. Parents who love each other have kids who love Jesus. The best thing a father can do for his son is the show him how much he loves his wife. The best thing a mother can do for her daughter is to show her how much she loves her husband. In this way, a young man learns how to love a woman. He learns how to be a husband. The mother teachers the daughter how to be a good wife in Jesus Christ.

When both the father and the mother, the husband and the wife, follow Christ, they release the wisdom and the Glory of God into their sons and daughters so that they too will follow in the steps of Jesus.

Parents must be consistent. This means parents must set reasonable rules and boundaries that are handled in the same way with each child over time in order to be fair to all. Most children enjoy the boundaries set for them. They may not express this, and they may test the boundaries, but they want to know if you are going to enforce what you say. Parents who are consistent in enforcing those rules and boundaries can actually end up becoming very close to their children.

This does not mean overdoing the rules or having rules without relationship. Relationship is first, and rules are second. Children will keep the rules because of the relationship, just as you keep the commandments of God because of your relationship with Jesus. There must always be room for exceptions to the rules and for forgiveness when those rules may be broken.

Please remember that your children's friends will influence or determine whether or not your child grows up to love Jesus. We become like the people we spend the most time with, so as a parent you need to monitor the friendships of your child. Your children need to be around other children who love Jesus just as you need Godly peers for friendship and encouragement. When worldly friendships become hurtful and detrimental, they need to be discouraged or even ended. Children are not always aware of who or what true friends are in their search for acceptance.

> **"In everything give thanks; for this is the will of God in Christ Jesus for you." 1 Thessalonians 5:18 (NKJV)**

> **"It is good to give thanks to the Lord, And to sing praises to Your name, O Most High;" Psalm 92: 1 (NKJV)**

Finally, teach your children an attitude of gratitude. This will release more of the presence of the Lord in their lives.

> *Another key to raising children in the Glory is to always treat them with the same love, kindness, and respect that the Lord Jesus shows to you!*

CHAPTER 15:

Supernatural Breakthroughs in the Glory

"And he said, 'Please show me Your glory.'"
Exodus 33:18 (NKJV)

Here, Moses was in the desert and he experienced what is called in theology, a *theophany*. A theophany is a God manifestation! When the Angel of the Lord appeared to Moses in the bush, the bush was burning, but the bush did not burn out. The scripture says that,

"For our God is a consuming fire." Hebrews 12:29 (KJV)

This bush that was burning, but never burned out, got Moses's attention and stirred his curiosity. One purpose for the Glory of God manifesting before your eyes is to get your attention and to stir your curiosity to find out more about who and what God is through His Son, Jesus Christ.

Moses began to find out the nature and the power of God's Glory through giving God his attention and curiosity. Curiosity will lead one into the revelation of who and what God is. Here, Moses asked God what His name was.

> **"And God said unto Moses, I AM THAT I AM: and He said, Thus shalt thou say unto the children of Israel, I AM hath sent me unto you." Exodus 3:14 (KJV)**

The Lord was saying, "I AM WHO I AM, I AM WHAT I AM, I WILL BE WHAT I WILL BE".

I believe it was the curiosity of Moses that brought this visitation of God Himself. Spiritual curiosity will bring you into a visitation of the Lord Jesus Christ. Intense spiritual hunger and curiosity will bring you into a revelation of WHO and WHAT GOD wants to be

to you, now, in your current situation through His Son, Jesus.The Father God is always looking for those who are curious. He is looking for those who seek a breakthrough in the WHO and WHAT GOD IS and how HE is to manifest HIMSELF in the here and the now!

> **"And looking at Jesus as He walked, he said, 'Behold the Lamb of God!'**
>
> **The two disciples heard him speak, and they followed Jesus. Then Jesus turned, and seeing them following, said to them, 'What do you**

seek?' They said to Him, 'Rabbi' (which is to say, when translated, Teacher), where are You staying?'

He said to them, 'Come and see.' They came and saw where He was staying, and remained with Him that day (now it was about the tenth hour)." John 1: 36-39 (NKJV)

Asking the right questions at the right time will cause you to have a revelation of where God is and where HE is manifesting HIMSELF! Asking the right question can cause you to have a breakthrough so that you can be in, and stay in, the NOW presence of God!

When the angel of God began to reveal who the Lord is, Moses got a breakthrough from his personal negativity. Moses had offered the Lord excuses why he could not go and be the deliverer of Israel.

"Then Moses answered and said, 'But suppose they will not believe me or listen to my voice; suppose they say, 'The Lord has not appeared to you.'" Exodus 4:1 (NKJV)

After he spent time in the presence of God, he was delivered of his low personal esteem, and he never brings it up again. He was definitely able to speak well by the Spirit and power of God.

One moment in the Glory of God can heal you of low personal esteem, negativity, rejection, hurt, and insecurity. God told Moses,

"...I will be certainly with you..." Exodus 3:12 (NKJV)

The manifestation of God's presence in Moses's life increased his confidence, his self-esteem was healed, his negativity was removed, and he was free to move in the Glory and power of God Almighty.

Right now, the presence of God is healing you of rejection, hurt, and in- security! Right now, you're getting a breakthrough from self-negativity by the supernatural presence and power of Jesus Christ!

"Now it came to pass in those days, when Moses was grown, that he went out to his brethren and looked at their burdens. And he saw an Egyptian beating a Hebrew, one of his brethren. So he looked this way and that way, and when he saw no one, he killed the Egyptian and hid him in the sand. And when he went out the second day, behold two Hebrew men were fighting, and he said to the one who did the wrong, 'Why are you striking your companion?'

Then he said, 'Who made you a prince and a judge over us? Do you intend to kill me as you killed the Egyptian?' So Moses feared and said, 'Surely this thing is known!'" Exodus 2:11-14 (NKJV)

Remember Moses had tried to deliver Israel from Egypt before and failed. When God's Glory was revealed to Moses, he was set free from his past failure! Regardless of the failure, you have experienced in the past, the Glory of God is setting you free now!

When God began to manifest Himself, Moses received a breakthrough from his current situation. In his current circumstances, he was a natural shepherd. However, by the anointing and the Glory, he was getting ready to be a *supernatural* shepherd. Through the power of God, he was going to set Israel free from captivity!

Right now, the things than have limited you are falling away because you are getting a breakthrough by the power and Glory of Jesus!

> **"Then He said, 'Do not draw near this place. Take your sandals off your feet, for the place where you stand is holy ground.'" Exodus 3:5 (NKJV)**

This means to take off your earth walk and leave it behind. You are getting ready to go someplace that you have never been to before. You are getting ready to go someplace you do not have a reference point for. It is time for your relationship with God to enter into a *supernatural realm* where you receive breakthroughs in the Glory! As you follow Jesus, you step into a heavenly walk where you will see signs, wonders, and miracles in answer to prayer in the name of Jesus!

Remember Moses grew up in Egypt, where there was extreme witchcraft. By the Glory and power of God, Moses was delivered from his former culture. There are people today who have been involved in psychic phenomena, reading horoscopes, Harry Potter, watching vampires, and werewolves. They have been involved in palm reading, watching horror movies, or paranormal activity. *If you or someone you know has been engaging in those demonic activities, it is time to repent, ask God for forgiveness, and receive a breakthrough from that dark activity by the name of Jesus, the power, and the Glory of God, right now!*

One of the reasons you have been in a state of frustration is because this is the place that you have been permitted to come to, so that you can have a breakthrough and a visitation from God. Frustration leads you into a fresh surrender to the living God! Through surrender, you are getting a breakthrough from mere head knowledge. What you know in your head has conformed you to your past.

> **"And do not be conformed to this world, but be transformed by the renewing of your mind, that you may prove what is the good and acceptable and perfect will of God." Romans 12:2 (NKJV)**

Information alone does not change you. It is the *revelation* from the Glory that brings transformation! The Glory of God is always releasing revelation from the throne of Jesus Christ.

Whatever you are conformed to, determines your reality. Your perception determines your reality. You have natural perception and you have supernatural perception. The supernatural move of God is based upon perception. The mind of Moses was transformed by the revelation of God's Word and the manifestation of God's Glory into his life. Your life and ministry will also be transformed as you receive revelation from God's Word and put it into practice. You too will see manifestations of the power and the Glory of Jesus!

Finally, the anointing and the Glory of God cause you to have a breakthrough from yourself. How far into the supernatural do you want to go? There are degrees of the supernatural. There is a difference between being born again and being filled with the Holy Spirit and speaking in other tongues. There is a difference between praying for a person to be healed of a headache, as opposed to praying for the blind to see, or the dead to be raised to life.

Whatever degree of supernatural you choose to walk into, it will require a level of commitment to Jesus. The Glory of God will lead you into holy dedication. You will rise no higher than your consecration to God. The greater your commitment to the Word of God, and the greater your consecration to follow Jesus, the greater will be the manifestations of the power and the Glory of God in your life and ministry.

> **"I beseech you therefore, brethren, by the mercies of God, that you present your bodies a living sacrifice, holy, acceptable to God, which is your reasonable service." Romans 12: 1 (NKJV)**

When you present your body as a living sacrifice (which means to offer up your life in exchange for living the Jesus life), you will move up into greater realms of the anointing and the Glory. When you deny yourself, take up your cross, and follow Jesus, you are giving worship to the Father. Because the Father of Glory is present, heaven is in continuous worship in the name of Jesus. When you deny yourself and follow Jesus, the Father of Glory is present in your life. Now you are in a realm of heaven, and you are constantly giving worship to the living God through your self-sacrifice, repentance, and obedience to the Word of the Lord!

When you obey the Word of the Lord, you are walking in the love of the Father. When you walk in the love of the Father, the Glory of God is revealed. When the Glory of God is perceived, the will of God is made known. When you act on the known will of God, you will see dramatic answers to prayer, healings, signs, wonders, and miracles! Take your breakthrough right now, by the Glory of God in the name of Jesus!

The key to supernatural breakthroughs in the Glory is dedication to the Word of God and a life consecrated to following Jesus!

CHAPTER 16:

Understanding the Glory

"But you shall receive power when the Holy Spirit has come upon you; and you shall be witnesses to Me in Jerusalem, and in all Judea and Samaria, and to the end of the earth." Acts 1: 8 (NKJV)

The Holy Spirit is the breath of God's Glory. The first thing Jesus says is you will receive the Holy Spirit, the Spirit of Glory. After you receive the SPIRIT of GOD'S GLORY, you will have power. Please notice the power comes after the Glory. The power is the gift of the Glory.

Many people bring to God the fruit of repentance, they practice righteousness, and they develop intimacy with Jesus. They start out in the Glory. In time, they begin to move in the gifts of the Glory, the anointing, and the power of the Spirit.

"For the gifts and the calling of God are without repentance." Romans 11: 29 (KJV)

The word *repentance* means *irrevocable*. Once God gives the gift, HE does not take it back. Sad to say, many people who start out in the Glory by obeying the Word of God, end up without the Glory because of sin. They continue in ministry because they retain the gift and power, even after losing the Glory.   If they do not repent, they will hear these words of Jesus,

"Many will say to me in that day, Lord, Lord, have we not prophesied in Your name? and in thy name cast out devils? And in thy name done many wonderful works? And then I will profess unto them, I never knew you; depart from me, ye that work iniquity." Matthew 7:22-23 (KJV)

When Jesus said these words "depart from me", it was the words of a Master Rabbi to a student (a disciple) who failed the final test! That person was dismissed and lost his relationship with his Master Rabbi.

It is by repentance, holiness, and intimacy with the FATHER, SON and HOLY SPIRIT that you step into the Glory. It is by obedience that you maintain that Glory and grow in the Glory, being conformed to the image and likeness of Jesus.

To walk in the Glory, in the way that is acceptable to the Father, is to walk in the Spirit and character of the Lord Jesus. We ask this question. Who is Jesus Christ? Jesus is the Son of God. Then we ask this question. What is

Jesus Christ? As to HIS character, JESUS is ALL of the fruit of the Holy Spirit.

> **"But the fruit of the Spirit is love, joy, peace, longsuffering, gentleness, goodness, faith, Meekness, temperance: against such there is no law." Galatians 5:22-23**

As to HIS ability, HE is ALL of the gifts of the Holy Spirit.

> **"For to one is given by the Spirit the word of wisdom; to another the word of knowledge by the same Spirit; To another faith by the same Spirit; to another gifts of healing by the same Spirit; To another the working of miracles; to another prophecy; to another discerning of spirits; to another divers kinds of tongues; to another the interpretation of tongues:" 1 Corinthians 12: 8-10 (KJV)**

He is EVERYTHING the WORD OF GOD says HE IS! Remember the Glory is more than an atmosphere. It is the essence, the nature, the ability, and all that the FATHER, the SON, and the HOLY SPIRIT are as the LORD GOD ALMIGHTY!

The more I walk in the unconditional love of God, the more I walk in the Glory. The more I walk in the peace and rest of the Father, the more I walk in the Glory of Jesus. When I walk in the joy of the Lord, I am walking in the joy of Jesus HIMSELF. The fruits of the Holy Spirit are expressions of the character and the Glory of the Father and Jesus!

"I say then: Walk in the Spirit, and you shall not fulfill the lust of the flesh." Galatians 5:16 (NKJV)

This means that I *submit* to the Spirit and *yield* to the Spirit. I *follow* the Spirit. I choose to *obey* the Spirit. I *walk within the limits and the boundaries* of the Holy Spirit. I stay *in the region* of the Spirit. I have decided to *live in the realm* of the Spirit. This is what the Glory life is all about in Jesus Christ!

If I walk in patience, one of the fruits of the Holy Spirit, Jesus makes me an overcomer by this quality of the Glory of God. The one person, the devil, cannot defeat is the one who walks in the fullness of the patience of Jesus.

"Truly the signs of an apostle were wrought among you in all patience, in signs, and wonders, and mighty deeds."
2 Corinthians 12: 12 (KJV)

What marked Paul as being a true and genuine apostle was not his signs, wonders and miracles, but it was how he walked in the patience of Jesus HIMSELF! If you read the whole chapter, you will first think that what qualified him to be an apostle was the miraculous, but the truth is, he said that he did these signs and wonders "in all patience"!

To walk in all patience is to walk in the fullness of the Glory of Jesus! The enemy fears you walking in the Glory fruit of Jesus more than the gifts of the Holy Spirit. The enemy has defeated the gifted, but he has never defeated those who walk in the full fruit of the Glory of God through yielding completely to Jesus. And, if you walk in the full fruit of God's Glory, the anointing, and the power of God's gifting, you will definitely be feared by the enemy. You will have the Glory of Jesus's character and the Glory of Jesus's divine ability! You will have a full-grown Jesus manifesting Himself through both your life and ministry. And, you will be a full-grown son or daughter of God through the full Glory of Jesus in your life and ministry!

"To them God willed to make known what are the riches of the glory of this mystery among the Gentiles: which is Christ in you, the hope of glory." Colossians 1: 27 (NKJV)

The key to understanding the Glory is to walk in the full fruit of God's Glory, the anointing, and the power of His gifting to you, always yielding completely to Him!

CHAPTER 17:

Prayer and Manifestations of the Glory

"Ask, and it will be given to you; seek, and you will find; knock, and it will be opened to you." Matthew 7: 7 (NKJV)

Jesus said that everyone who asks, receives; everyone who seeks, finds; for everyone who knocks at the door, the door shall be opened.

Kathryn Kuhlman had her own entrance to the Pittsburgh airport because people would fall out under the presence and power of the Holy Spirit when she walked in. At first, the authorities wondered why people would just suddenly collapse to the floor. Then, they figured out it that this was a woman of God, so they gave her a personal entrance at this airport. The story is also told that as she walked through a kitchen at a hotel, different people collapsed under the presence and power of the Holy Spirit.

It was said that Charles Finney walked into a factory on a typical work day in up-state New York. What happened? Heaven walked in! Everyone in the factory began to weep in the presence of God all at once. Why? Because the man carried a lifestyle of prayer, and the presence of God was on and all around him. This presence impacted people.

There is a place in India called Kerala. While traveling outside the Roman Empire to preach the gospel, the apostle Thomas went there to observe the Brahmin priests. They would worship the sun by throwing water up in the air, and then it would fall back down. The apostle observed this for three days. After three days, he walked down to the priests and said, "Why doesn't your God receive your sacrifice?"

They said, "What do you mean?"

He said, "You throw water up to your sun god as a sacrifice, but he doesn't receive it. It just falls back down to you."

After that the apostle Thomas presented a challenge to them and said, "I'm going to pray to *my* God, and when I do, I will throw water up in the air, and it will remain suspended in the air."

Of course, they were totally skeptical. Thomas said, "Lord, I've seen you face-to-face and thank you for signs and wonders." Thomas threw the water into the air and the water remained suspended in midair for three days!

Every single one of the Brahmin priests were born again and followed the way of Jesus! The whole area was swept into the good news and to this day, it is the most Christian region in all of India! Thomas needed a tangible experience, and that tangible experience anchored him into a world-changing message. That message impacted the region he worked in, not just for a moment, but for generations to come!

T.L. Osborne was a missionary in India. In fact, he was a failed missionary. He would go and bring the scriptures with nothing else. The people would not receive his words. Burnt out and discouraged, he moved back to America. After coming back to the States to pastor a small church, he was down-trodden, depressed, and thinking about quitting the ministry altogether.

In the summer of 1949, in Portland, Oregon, his wife went to a William Branham meeting. (Branham was an American Christian minister and faith healer who began the post-World War II healing revival.) Afterwards, she told her husband about the meeting. He was reluctant to go but finally

decided to say yes. He saw the prophet minister to a deaf and mute boy who was completely healed in the meeting! Osborne felt like God spoke to him and said, "You could do that!"

Osborne went home and fasted for three days and three nights. He had no bread and no water. Jesus appeared to him and said, "I am the same yesterday, today, and forever." After that he began a miracle-working ministry. He was known for demonstrating the supernatural power of a living God!

Walter was a teacher at a Bible college. The students came to class one day, and the presence of God started to fall and that presence remained. Classes were suspended for ten days because of the manifest presence of God!

> **"Be still, and know that I am God; I will be exalted among the nations, I will be exalted in the earth!" Psalm 46: 10 (NKJV)**

The Hebrew for *be still* means *to let go*. Let go and know I AM! When Christians let go of anxiety while seeking GOD and rest, HIS GLORY falls!

Once while I was doing a meeting in the state of Tennessee, a man was struck down on the floor and vibrated for forty-five minutes. Because of a manifestation of the Glory of God, Jesus was seen in the meeting!

In another meeting, the Glory of God came into the service, and a young woman in the Baptist church had her feet stuck to the floor at the altar until after the meeting was over. When the Glory of God lifted off of her, she was actually able to leave the church and go home.

At a different meeting, a woman, who was slain in the Spirit, felt an angel sit on her. Her body was so heavy she could

not rise up. When the Glory lifted, she was finally able to get up.

When I was doing a Supernatural School, the presence of God was so strong that anyone who came up to the altar area fell out under the power of God.

Charles Finney prayed until Jesus appeared to him.

John Wesley told the Lord that he was going to read the book of Ephesians one hundred times. On the hundredth time, he looked up and saw Jesus staring at him! That encounter sparked the Great Awakening, a widespread revival that led to the establishment of the Methodist Church.

A great prophet was spending time with Jesus, wanting to walk in signs and wonders desperately. He prayed, paced, rocked, and sought the Lord. For extended periods of time, he cried out to God to move by the power of the Holy Spirit.

Finally, one day, he was taken up in a vision with Jesus to the Father's throne. He heard the Father say to him, "Son, what do you want?"

He cried out with as loud a voice as possible, "I want to move in signs and wonders!"

The Lord responded, "Son, what do you want?"

Not understanding why God wasn't hearing him, he said again, "I want to move in signs and wonders!"

God responded with the same question. "Son, what is it you want?"

Finally, he cried out with the same voice, "God, I want you!"

When he declared that, God began to laugh, not just a laugh, but a belly laugh.

In that moment, something like a fire came out of the throne and hit this man in his chest. He fell back into his own body. The Glory of God was surging through him, and he knew he had seen God face-to-face and would never be the same!

The next

week, miracles began to happen! Missing limbs began to grow back! There was an outbreak of signs and wonders that became normal in his meetings. Why? Because in the secret place, he didn't merely pursue miracles and the power of God, but he desired GOD HIMSELF!

> **"...and lo, I am with you always, even to the end of the age." Matthew 28:20 (NKJV)**
>
> **"So He said, 'I will certainly be with you...'" Exodus 3:12 (NKJV)**
>
> **"...as I was with Moses, so I will be with you. I will not leave you nor forsake you." Joshua 1: 5 (NKJV)**
>
> *The key to prayer and God's power is to look for GOD HIMSELF, not just His manifestations of power! When you find the GOD OF GLORY, HE WILL manifest HIMSELF with power in the name of JESUS!*

CHAPTER 18:

Ministry Keys of the Glory

All manifestations of God need an *anchor*. The *instruction* or the Word of God is the anchor! The *inspiration* for manifestation should be the Word of God. What maintains the manifestation of God is HIS WORD.

A message without manifestation will eventually lead to doubt and unbelief. The message that puts the acts of God in the past or in the future, but never in the present, will lead people to believe that God does not do the miraculous today.

The message with the manifestation leads to a magnifying and glorifying of the Lord Jesus Christ! When you see the manifestation, the revelation becomes a reality before your eyes.

"Jesus Christ is the same yesterday, today, and forever." Hebrew 13:8 (NKJV)

That means if Jesus did miracles yesterday, Jesus does miracles today, and Jesus will be doing miracles tomorrow! When a minister teaches the Word of God, but does not believe that there will be any manifestation following, then the people come to that same belief.

> "In this manner, therefore, pray: Our Father in heaven, Hallowed be Your name. Your kingdom come. Your will be done On earth as it is in heaven. Give us this day our daily bread. And forgive us our debts, As we forgive our debtors. And do not lead us into temptation, But deliver us from the evil one. For Yours is the kingdom and the power and the glory forever. Amen." Matthew 6: 9- 13 (NKJV)

Jesus says that you are to pray for His Kingdom to come and His will to be done. You are to say to God, "Yours is the Kingdom (*the message*), the power (*the manifestation*), and the glory (*the movement*)."The message or the Word of God produces the manifestation or the power of God. When you have continuous manifestation, it creates a movement or the Glory of God!

> "And I, brethren, when I came to you, did not come with excellence of speech or of wisdom declaring to you the testimony of God. For I determined not to know anything among you except Jesus Christ and Him crucified. I was with you in weakness, in fear, and in much trembling. And my speech and my preaching were not with persuasive words of human wisdom, but in demonstration of the Spirit and

of power, that your faith should not be in the wisdom of men but in the power of God." 1 Corinthians 2: 1-5 (NKJV)

Here the apostle Paul says that he did not come with excellence of speech or wisdom when he gave the brethren the Word of God, God's testimony, but he was with them in weakness, fear, and much trembling. His speech was not with great skill but his preaching was of Jesus Christ. It was accompanied by the moving of the Spirit and the power of God so that their faith would not stand in the wisdom of men but in the power of God.

"For the kingdom of God is not in word but in power." 1 Corinthians 4: 20 (NKJV)

Paul would make a DECLARATION of the WORD OF GOD, and that would be accompanied by a DEMON-STRATION OF THE HOLY SPIRIT and POWER!

There are times that it is the will of God for us to have manifestations after the Word of God has been revealed, but it is not wise for us to build ministries upon supernatural manifestations. If a ministry is built on supernatural manifestations or the gifts of the Holy Spirit, people would judge the meetings by the number of signs displayed or the quality of the signs that are a part of the service. In one way or another, there is the distinct possibility that people could put the minister under great pressure to perform.

While it is true that different manifestations actually meet the needs of people, manifestations do not bring people into maturity. It is the revelation and application of the Word of God that bring people to maturity and fullness through Jesus!

> **"But be doers of the word, and not hearers only, deceiving yourselves." James 1: 22 (NKJV)**

> **"But whoever keeps His word, truly the love of God is perfected in him. By this we know that we are in Him." 1 John 2:5 (NKJV)**

The same scripture in the Message translation makes the point even more clear.

> **"If someone claims, 'I know him well!' but doesn't keep his commandments, he's obviously a liar. His life doesn't match his words. But the one who keeps God's word is the person in whom we see God's mature love. This is the only way to be sure we're in God. Anyone who claims to be intimate with God ought to live the same kind of life Jesus lived." 1 John 2: 5-6 (MSG)**

In other words, when a person obeys God that person loves God completely. Allow me to urge you to build your life and ministry on the revelation and the application of God's Word.

> **"And Jesus went about all Galilee, teaching in their synagogues, preaching the gospel of the kingdom, and healing all kinds of sickness and all kinds of disease among the people." Matthew 4:23 (NKJV)**

Jesus preached the Word of God and taught the Word of God in the synagogues, and after that, He healed every kind of sickness and every kind of disease among the people!

"Jesus replied, 'You are in error because you do not know the Scriptures or the power of God.'" Matthew 22:29 (NIV)

Jesus told some religious leaders that the reason that they were in error or mistaken was because they did not know the scriptures or the power of God.

Jesus was saying that there had to be a marriage between the Word of God and the Holy Spirit. The truth of the matter is that in some circles there has been a DIVORCE between the WORD and the SPIRIT. It is obvious that Jesus struck a BALANCE between the WORD and the SPIRIT ministry. I think that we go into error if our ministry is *only* the WORD or if it is *only* the SPIRIT.

"Then He said to them, 'Follow Me, and I will make you fishers of men.'" Matthew 4:19 (NKJV)

If we are to FOLLOW JESUS in ministry, then we need to have a ministry that marries the WORD with the SPIRIT, the SCRIPTURES with the POWER OF GOD.

"Then Jesus was led by the Spirit into the wilderness to be tempted by the devil. And when He had fasted forty days and forty nights, afterward He was hungry. Now when the tempter came to him, he said, 'If you are

the son of God, command that these stones become bread.' But He answered and said, 'It is written...'" Matthew 4: 1-4 (NKJV)

Temptation is never the ground for a manifestation! In the book of Matthew, chapter 4, and the book of Luke, chapter 4, Jesus was tempted by the devil in the beginning of His ministry. He answered him with the Word, not with a manifestation of His power.

"And when Jesus went out He saw a great multitude; and He was moved with compassion for them, and healed their sick." Matthew 14: 14 (NKJV)

According to the Word of God, obedience to the Father and the Glory of Jesus are the grounds for manifestation. This means the compassion of Christ is grounds for manifestation. It means the desire to serve others in the Spirit of Christ is grounds for manifestation!

The key to ministry in the Glory is the love and compassion of Christ that releases the power and the manifestations. LOVE RELEASES the GLORY!

CHAPTER 19:

How to Build the Cloud of God's Glory

"And the Lord went before them by day in a pillar of cloud to lead the way, and by night in a pillar of fire to give them light, so as to go by day and night. He did not take away the pillar of cloud by day or the pillar of fire by night from before the people." Exodus 13: 21-22 (NKJV)

"And it came to pass when the priests came out of the Most Holy Place (for all the priests who were present had sanctified themselves, without keeping to their divisions), and the Levites who were the singers, all those of Asaph and Heman and Jeduthun, with their sons and their brethren, stood at the east end of the altar, clothed in white linen, having cymbals, stringed instruments and harps, and with them one hundred and twenty priests sounding the trumpets---indeed it came to pass, when the trumpeters and singers were as one, to make one sound to be heard in praising and thanking the Lord, and when they lifted up their voice with the trumpets and cymbals and instruments of music, and praised the Lord, saying:

'For He is good, For His mercy endures forever,'

That the house, the house of the Lord, was filled with a cloud, so that the priests could not continue ministering because of the cloud; for the glory of the Lord filled the house of God." 2 Chronicles 5: 11-14 (NKJV)

"But You are holy, Enthroned in the praises of Israel." Psalm 22:3 (NKJV)

"Now it came to pass, about eight days after these sayings, that He took Peter, John, and James and went up on the mountain to pray. As He prayed, the appearance of his face was altered, and His robe became white and glistening. And behold, two men talked with Him, who were Moses and Elijah, who appeared in glory and spoke of his decease which He was about to accomplish at Jerusalem. But Peter and those with him were heavy with sleep; and when they were fully awake, they saw His glory and the two men who stood with Him. Then it happened, as they were parting from him, that Peter said to Jesus, 'Master, it is good for us to be here; and let us make three tabernacles: one for You, one for Moses, and one for Elijah'---not knowing what he said.

While he was saying this, a cloud came and overshadowed them; and they were fearful as they entered the cloud. And a voice came out of the cloud, saying, 'This is My beloved Son. Hear Him!'" Luke 9: 28-35 (NKJV)

In order to access the GLORY of the FATHER, one's prayer must be more than words. It must be the actual sacrifice of oneself in exchange for the life of Jesus and the will of God. The cloud is the manifestation of the presence and the Glory of God.

There are old clouds and new clouds; old manifestations and new manifestations of God's presence and Glory. There are times when it must be understood that the old cloud has dried up, and it is diminishing. The old cloud is no longer producing the life that it once did. Just as when you first hear a new song, there is an anointing and a glory that is in that song. However, six months later, the anointing, and the glory that was in that song begins to diminish. Now you are looking for a new song to bring a new cloud and a new glory.

When the cloud of God's presence comes into a meeting, there will be a manifestation of God's Glory! Each believer has his own cloud. No one can create a cloud for you. *You* need to create your own cloud to function in. Every believer needs to know that when you pray, praise, and worship Jesus, the Spirit of God makes your cloud or manifestation of God's Glory.

> **"And they were calling to one another: 'Holy, holy, holy is the Lord Almighty; the whole earth is full of his glory.' At the sound of their voices the doorposts and thresholds shook and the temple was filled with smoke." Isaiah 6:3 (NIV)**

The Word of God says that as the angels were calling out, the temple of God in heaven was filled with smoke or a cloud.

> **"And the smoke of the incense, which came with the prayers of the saints, ascended up before God out of the angel's hand." Revelation 8: 4 (NKJV)**

The angel of God offered incense and there was a smoke and a cloud that arose before God with the prayers of the saints that came from the hand of the angel near the altar of God before the holy throne.

In a church service, when all of the believers are praising and worshiping the Father in the name of Jesus, the individual clouds come together when the service reaches a climax. As we worship Jesus and the Father, God will start to manifest what is in the cloud of His Glory.

If there is no manifestation, it is because of the following reasons:

- The clouds are empty. The word of God talks about clouds without water. Also, every single one of us have seen clouds in the sky but they have had no water, and so, they could give forth no rain.

- Sometimes we fail to discern

- what the cloud of God's glory is there for!

- Sometimes there is not a "know how" of how to get the cloud to rain what is needed.

- Sometimes we did not pray, praise and worship enough to seed the cloud for what is needed. What is in the CLOUD is determined by the promises of GOD you are believing HIM to rain down on you. You want to be a part of the prayer, praise, and worship in a service because you want to be a part of forming the cloud, the Glory! According to your faith, what you are believing for is in the cloud and will rain upon you.

There are also times when you will receive unexpected blessings and surprise miracles because of the cloud that is present. In the CLOUD of GLORY, you minister the WORD, and the CLOUD carries your voice. What you begin to talk about in the Word of God begins to manifest and take on form, shape, substance, and matter by the Glory and power of God!

In the cloud, the Glory, there is no time, distance, or space in the realm of the Holy Spirit.

"After this I looked, and behold, a door opened in heaven: and the first voice which I heard was as it were of a trumpet talking with me; which said, Come up hither, and I will shew thee things which must be hereafter. And immediately I was in the Spirit: and, behold, a throne was set in heaven, and one sat on the throne." Revelation 4:1-2 (KJV)

Your worship reveals where you are. The apostle John heard a voice that said to him, come up here, and the apostle said, *immediately,* I was in the Spirit. Your worship can open a door in heaven. Keep your worship fresh and know God in the now.

When you worship the Father, the Spirit of God stands beside you and creates the cloud of Glory. This is why there are times when you will see the move of God in certain parts of the sanctuary and not in other parts of the sanctuary.

If you do not keep your worship fresh and sing the songs of the Lord, the prophetic songs, you will lose the cloud. Your praise and worship determine the measurement of the cloud, the presence, and the Glory. If your praise and worship are always the same old songs, you will find yourself in a rut. What was a big cloud is now getting smaller and smaller. This is why it must be *fresh worship* given by the inspiration of the Spirit.

You will continue to need a fresh revelation of God through his Word because continuing revelation perpetuates the cloud, the presence, and the Glory. Your revelation determines the cloud. Old revelations produce old clouds and new revelations produce new clouds of the Glory! Revelation is the means by which we perceive the cloud, the presence, and what is in the Glory.

Before the Lord Jesus returns, the worship of the saints on earth will line up with the worship of the saints in heaven. There is a corporate ascending into God's Glory in a church service, and the truth is we do not all get there at the same time. In the corporate service, the ascent into the presence and into the Glory of God is by sequence.

First, the outer court, the place of faith. You ascend by the power of the blood of Jesus. Then you begin to pray in the Holy Spirit until you enter thanksgiving and praise! Now you are in the inner court. You give thanks, and you praise God until you reach a higher level of the anointing. You move from the realm of the anointing until you enter into the realm of the Glory! Now you are in the holy of holies where GOD IS, and where HE MANIFESTS HIMSELF!

It is important to press past the realm of the anointing until you move into the realm of the GLORY and you have manifestations of the GLORY! The realm of your anointing is the realm of your gifting where you work. In the realm of GOD'S' GLORY, you do not work. You rest, and God does the work! As you worship, GOD does the work all by HIMSELF in the NAME of JESUS!

In the anointing, you may pray for someone; in the Glory, you do not pray for individuals. The individual receives from the person and presence of God directly without the laying on of hands.

In the anointing, you may lay hands on a person, and he may receive from God through your personal ministry. In the Glory, you get the person to believe the WORD OF GOD, receive from His PRESENCE, and be touched by the HAND of God. By the GLORY, you bypass the hand of man and go directly to the hand of GOD.

In the anointing, you can minister to a few, but in the GLORY, God can minister to many.

In the anointing, Jesus works through you, but in the Glory, Jesus works without you.

If there is warfare during prayer, thanksgiving, praise, or worship, it is because you have not ascended high enough into the Glory of God. You have to use praise and worship to ascend beyond principalities, powers, rulers of darkness, and spiritual wickedness in high places to manifest the GLORY OF GOD upon the earth. If you do not praise and worship high enough, you will feel a heaviness in the service.

You must praise and worship God until there is a supernatural breakthrough of the Glory. In the Glory, arthritis, cancer, sickness, disease, restrictions, debts, and bondages can be destroyed as you enter the Glory and the power of God during your praise and worship of the FATHER and JESUS.

In the cloud of GOD's GLORY, every Spirit-filled believer receives a word, a revelation, a prophecy, or a vision. When you are in the GLORY you can have spiritual perceptions or "knowings" from God. You can have heavenly experiences and trances. You can see angels and the Lord Jesus! In the cloud of GLORY, your spiritual perception is reality.

Revelation knowledge is within the cloud. Sometimes the cloud lifts and you have to pray, praise, and worship until that cloud comes back into the service. When the Glory cloud returns, it may not be the same realm of Glory. Now you have to minister out of the present cloud.

The greater the praise and worship, the greater the cloud and the move of God. Praise and worship release the angels of God. Your praise and worship cause the breath of the heavens, the GLORY of God to enter the service. *Your praise and worship advance you to the level of GLORY where GOD will manifest what HE wants to say to you, what HE wants to do for you and what HE wants to do in you!*

When you call forth what is in the GLORY, it will manifest. You cannot call forth what is not in the GLORY at that time. However, when you say what you perceive in the CLOUD and the GLORY, it is created. When you CALL IT OUT of the cloud, IT IS CREATED, IN THE NAME OF JESUS!

What may be in the CLOUD? Salvation, healing, deliverance, the baptism in the Holy Spirit, revival, renewal, refreshing, prosperity, gifting, anointing, ministry callings, creativity, comfort, confidence caring, courage, government, change, conviction, repentance correction, direction, holiness, revelations, visitation, and/or the miraculous!

One word rightly discerned can use up the atmosphere of the GLORY OF GOD and meet the needs of the people. It can cause the Kingdom of God to come, and GOD's will to be done. Once you have used up the atmosphere of the GLORY, you must begin to build again the cloud through prayer, praise, and worship.

There are two kinds of GLORY. There is a *temple GLORY* which is a permanent or resident GLORY. And, there is a *tabernacle GLORY* which is temporary and a moving GLORY.

When you are looking at a resident GLORY, you have to constantly build an atmosphere. You must educate the people to the atmosphere so that the people's personal life will correspond to the GLORY that is there. The crowd affects the cloud, and when people understand the cloud, then the cloud impacts the crowd.

The moving GLORY requires that you discern the movement of the cloud. It means that you must be willing to change and go with the GLORY. It means that you must adapt and adjust. You must change your plans to follow the GLORY and choose to be led by the GLORY.

The key to building the cloud of God's Glory is true praise and worship of the Father!

CHAPTER 20:

Cycles of Spirit, Life, and Glory

"For therein is the righteousness of God revealed from faith to faith: as it is written, The just shall live by faith." Romans 1: 17 (KJV)

"So then faith cometh by hearing, and hearing by the word of God." Romans 10:17 (KJV)

In the original language, this means that *faith is by the report but the report is by the utterance of God.* The Father of faith is the Word of God. What gives birth to faith is the Word of the Lord. When there is no Word, there is no faith. When there is a little bit of the Word, there is a little bit of faith. A person's degree of faith is dependent upon the revelation of the Word.

"For I say, through the grace given to me, to everyone who is among you, not to think of himself more highly than he ought to think, but

to think soberly, as God has dealt to each one a measure of faith." Romans 12:3 (NKJV)

Where a person has revelation, that is where they have faith! Where a person's revelation stops, that is where his faith stops. You cannot have faith beyond your revelation. Revelation is the jurisdiction of your faith.

Where your faith is, that is where your anointing is! Where your anointing is, that is your lead into the GLORY! That means the limit of your faith is determined by the limit of your revelation. The reason you run out of faith is because you have run out of revelation. When you run out of revelation, you come to the end of that faith.

The scripture makes it clear:

"For in it the righteousness of God is revealed from faith to faith..." Romans 1: 17 (NKJV)

You grow from revelation to revelation. You grow from faith to faith. It takes an on-going revelation to have an on-going faith. When you do not have an on-going revelation, you get stuck in your faith and stay there. You repeat your past, but you do not move forward with the cloud!

Just as revelation determines your faith, your faith will determine your experience. Without continuing revelation, you will experience the same events over and over again, even when GOD wants to give you a new experience by the revelation and faith of HIS SON, JESUS!

"Beloved, while I was very diligent to write to you concerning our common salvation, I found it necessary to write to you to contend earnestly for the faith which was once for all delivered to the saints." Jude 3: 1 (NKJV)

The apostle says that he wants to encourage you to *contend for the faith* which was once delivered to the saints. The word *contend* means to *fight for and maintain*. In order for you to experience the dynamic development of the Holy Spirit in your life and move from faith to faith, you must contend for a greater revelation to have a greater faith, a greater intimacy, and a greater experience with God and in Jesus Christ! A greater revelation, a greater glory!

"They go from strength to strength; Each one appears before God in Zion." Psalm 84: 7 (NKJV)

You can move from one level of ANOINTING to ANOTHER DEGREE OF ANOINTING by the revelation and faith of God's Word. I challenge you to CONTEND for a new ANOINTING IN YOUR DAY!

"But we all, with veiled face, beholding as in a mirror the glory of the Lord, are being transformed into the same image from glory to glory, just as by the Spirit of the Lord." 2 Corinthians 3; 18 (NKJV)

When you put application to your revelation by FAITH, the ANOINTING empowers you to move from GLORY TO GLORY by the SPIRIT OF THE LIVING GOD! I urge you to CONTEND FOR THE GLORY OF GOD that HE wants to pour out and reveal for your generation.

Some of you have been wondering why you are under such pressure, and going through trials and tribulations. The purpose may be to make you move from a place of contentment to a place of contending!

You have a choice. You can stay in the cycle of your contentment, your present or past achievements, or you can break into a new realm of revelation and manifestation. You can begin a brand-new cycle by faith with the anointing and the Glory!

After you have experienced the new and have come into a dynamic development of the SPIRIT, you experience the MOVE of God. The next phase you enter is a period of MAINTENANCE. Whatever it is the Lord has done, you must guard it, protect it, and keep it.

Please understand that before the next period of advancement, temptation will come to turn you back to what was. The thoughts, words, actions, and reactions of the past must be resisted. When the cycle of temptation is resisted, then you enter into the next phase of dynamic development by the Spirit of God. Emergencies, crises, pressure, and trials are designed to distract you and detour you from the path God has laid before you to keep you from entering into new places of faith, anointing, and Glory!

This cycle of development and maintenance is the pathway into new realms of faith, the anointing and the Glory. These are the ways of the Holy Spirit!

"When all the people were baptized, it came to pass that Jesus was also baptized; and while He prayed, the heaven was opened. And the Holy Spirit descended in bodily form like a dove upon Him, and a voice came from heaven which said, 'You are My beloved Son; in You I am well pleased.'" Luke 3: 21-22

First, Jesus receives the Holy Spirit. Then, heaven opens, and finally, HE hears the voice of the FATHER. This is *dynamic development*.

Next, Jesus goes into the desert to fast and pray. HE is led by the Holy Spirit to do so, after HE has been filled with the Holy Spirit.

"Then Jesus, being filled with the Holy Spirit, returned from the Jordan and was led by the Spirit into the wilderness," Luke 4: 1 (NKJV)

First, Jesus receives the Spirit, then, Jesus is full of the Spirit, and finally, Jesus is led by the Spirit to fast and pray.

Now the enemy comes with different trials and temptations. Jesus enters a phase of *maintenance*.

"Then Jesus returned in the power of the Spirit to Galilee, and news of Him went out through all the surrounding region." Luke 4: 14 (NKJV)

When Jesus maintains what HE received by the SPIRIT, HE enters into another phase of dynamic development. The scripture says Jesus *returned in the power of the Holy Spirit.* In other words, first, JESUS experiences dynamic development, then, HE maintains what HE receives, and finally, HE gets an *upgrade* from the FATHER through the Holy Spirit.

There are differences between a cycle and a circle. It can be a cycle and a *circle of the flesh*, or it can be a cycle and a *circle of the SPIRIT.* When it is a circle of the *flesh,* there will be no growth but a circling back of the same trials and temptations.

If it is a cycle and a circle of *the Spirit,* you will see a divine upgrade. There will be growth and expansion as you walk in faith, obedience, and patience by Jesus.

> *The key to being UPGRADED by the FATHER is to maintain what HE gives you when you experience the dynamic development of the SPIRIT!*

CHAPTER 21:

Seasons and the Glory

"To everything there is a season, A time for every purpose under heaven:" Ecclesiastes 3: 1 (NKJV)

You have one purpose, but you have many seasons. A person can have a season of silence, trials, blessings, frustrations, or many other things. But, the Holy Spirit will always give you a song for every season that you are walking through.

When you are walking through the season of the desert, be sure not to lose your song.

"Then Israel sang this song:

'Spring up, O well! All of you sing to it---The well the leaders sank, Dug by the nation's nobles, By the lawgiver, with their staves.'

And from the wilderness they went to Mattanah,"

Numbers 21: 17-18 (NKJV)

Here, the sons of Israel needed water. They were told by God to sing this song," Spring up, O well". The word *spring* in the Hebrew means *to ascend*. In other words, they were telling God that the water hidden in the earth needed to ascend and come forth to give them a supernatural supply. It was both a prayer and a prediction by the Spirit of God!

There is a song for every season! And, in that song given by the Holy Spirit, there's a supernatural supply in the name of Jesus!

Your heavenly FATHER also provides angels for every season. For every season, there is an angel assigned to bring the manifestation of JESUS and to give GLORY to GOD the FATHER.

"And He said, 'Hagar, Sarai's maid, where have you come from, and where are you going?'

She said, 'I am fleeing from the presence of my mistress Sarai.'

The Angel of the Lord said to her, 'Return to your mistress, and submit yourself under her hand.' Then the Angel of the Lord said to her, 'I will multiply your descendants exceedingly, so that they shall be counted for multitude.' And the Angel of the Lord said to her:

'Behold, you are with child, And you shall bear a son. You shall call his name Ishmael, Because the Lord has heard your affliction. He shall be a wild man; his hand shall be against every man, And every man's hand against him. And he shall dwell in the presence of all his brethren.'

Then she called the name of the Lord who spoke to her, You-Are-the-God-Who-Sees; for she said, 'Have I also here seen him who sees me?'" Genesis 16: 8- 13 (NKJV)

Hagar was a woman alone in a desert. She ran out of water for her child, and she began to pray to God who sent an angel to her. She received a supernatural supply of water, and she called the name of the place, "the Lord who sees me". Notice that the *angel of the Lord found her*. That means that God sends an angel to find *you* in your season to give *you* a supernatural supply, in the name of Jesus!

Here is a testimony. A man is in a car accident. The angel opens up the door and tells the man he would be healed, and to completely disregard the report of the medical staff. The medical staff said that the man's leg needed to be amputated. The man believed the Word of God instead, and he was completely healed!

Another testimony: There was a woman who had three different kinds of cancer. The angel of God appeared to her and told her that she would be healed. It came to pass just as God had said!

"But at night an angel of the Lord opened the prison doors and brought them out, ..." Acts 5: 19 (NKJV)

The angel supernaturally brought the 12 apostles out of prison.

"Now behold, an angel of the Lord stood by him, and a light shone in the prison; and he struck Peter on the side and raised him up, saying 'Arise quickly!' And his chains fell off his hands. Then the angel said to him, 'Put on your garment and follow me.' So he went out and followed him, and did not know that what was done by the angel was real, but thought he was seeing a vision. When they were past the first and second guard posts, they came to the iron gate that leads to the city, which opened to them of its own accord; and they went out and went down one street, and immediately the angel departed from him." Acts 12: 7- 10 (NKJV)

Peter was about to be killed, but the angel of the Lord delivers him out of the hand of his enemy.

"And the Angel of the Lord appeared to the woman and said to her, 'Indeed now, you are barren and have bourne no children, but you shall conceive and bear a son.'" Judges 13:3 (NKJV)

A woman could not have a child. God sends an angel, she is healed, and this woman gives birth to Samson, a mighty man of God, supernaturally!

> **"So Cornelius said, 'Four days ago I was fasting until this hour; and at the ninth hour I prayed in my house, and behold, a man stood before me in bright clothing, and said, 'Cornelius, your prayer has been heard, and your alms are remembered in the sight of God.. Send therefore to Joppa and call Simon here, whose surname is Peter....'" Acts 10: 30-32 (NKJV)**

> **"While Peter was still speaking these words, the Holy Spirit fell upon all those who heard the word." Acts 10: 44 (NKJV)**

Here, the angel of God visits Cornelius, and as a result, Peter ends up at his house, and the man and his family and friends are saved in Jesus's name!

The Lord has angels for all seasons. *Release your faith towards God right now, and ask Him to send an angel so that you can have a seasonal change, in the name of Jesus!* The Lord will deal with you and visit you, according to the season of life that you are in right now!

> **"When the morning dawned, the angels urged Lot to hurry, saying, 'Arise, take your wife and your two daughters who are here, lest you be consumed in the punishment of the city.' And while he lingered, the men took hold of his hand, his wife's hand, and the hands of his two daughters, the Lord being merciful to him, and**

they brought him out and set him outside the city." Genesis 19: 15-16 (NKJV)

The Lord sent angels, and Lot and his family were directed and escorted to safety.

The key to moving into a new season is new revelation and a new visitation, in the name of Jesus! A new revelation can take you into a new experience of GOD'S GLORY!

CHAPTER 22:

Overcoming Insecurity in the Glory

"I have set the Lord always before me; Because He is at my right hand I shall not be moved." Psalm 16: 8 (NKJV)

When a person is struggling with insecurity, this is what they say to themselves, "What is wrong with me"? The focus of insecurity is self-doubt. The enemy uses insecurity to rob you of personal confidence. In- security means you are not confident about your worth in your eyes, in the eyes of others, or even in the eyes of God.

While you may have a desire to minister to others, it is really hard to do so effectively and powerfully when you doubt yourself. You doubt the worth of your words. You doubt that others have confidence in you and you may even doubt that Jesus believes in you. This kind of self-negativity can hinder you from believing that you can actually represent Jesus. Insecurity can make you so self-conscience that it can block your ability to hear from God. You doubt that what you heard came from God, and it can block the flow of the anointing to you and through you.

Insecurity will create anxiety and fear about your relationships. And, ministry is all about positive relationships! Insecurity and self-negativity will cause you to fear rejection from others and generate a deep uncertainty about whether your feelings or desires, including ministry feelings or desires, are legitimate. Self-negativity and insecurity make you feel illegitimate. As a result of the self-negativity and insecurity, you may experience self-rejection and even depression. Because of the negative things that you have been told about yourself, such as personal weaknesses, maybe your lack of education, a lack of financial status, your personal appearance, your past perceived and/or real failures, you may have self-negativity and insecurity.

When you suffer from self-negativity, the fear of the loss of approval, the loss of wanting everyone to love and accept you, and the loss of potential favor from others is very painful. To focus on what is wrong with you ties you to the earth and makes it difficult for you to move in the supernatural, to maintain a supernatural life full of peace and joy, or to minister in the supernatural.

Insecurity keeps you in a state of self-consciousness, but you must be *God-conscious* to step into the supernatural and minister from there. The self-negativity that drives insecurity will undermine the authenticity of your genuine authority and faith in the supernatural ability of God to work through you. Self-negativity and insecurity will feed your fear and anxiety.

> **"The Lord is my light and my salvation; Whom shall I fear? The Lord is the strength of my life; Of whom shall I be afraid?"**
> **Psalm 27: 1 (NKJV)**

When the prophet, Samuel, came to David's father looking for the next King of Israel, David was so disregarded by his father and his brothers that he was not even called to the dinner! Here is a picture of a young man being rejected by the very people who should love him and accept him. It is obvious that there was a degree of negativity toward David. How fascinating it is that the very one they rejected is the very one

God chose!

The very fact that you have been rejected, hurt, abandoned, neglected, or even mentally, emotionally, or otherwise abused means that you are the very one that God is choosing in this hour because HE loves you so much, in the name of Jesus!

Apparently, the prophet David forgave his father and his brothers. The Lord became his light and saved him from self-negativity and insecurity by the power of the Holy Spirit. David goes on to say that the Lord is the strength of his life. It was the love and acceptance of God that gave strength to David so that he came into a place of security because of the favor and grace of the Lord's presence in his life.

David did not look at the rejection of his father and his brother. Instead, he looked at the love and acceptance of God in his life.

> **"I have set the Lord always before me; Because He is at my right hand I shall not be moved." Psalm 16: 8 (NKJV)**

David looked to the Lord because who You look to determines how you feel! You can *choose* to look to the person or the people who are negative toward you and be hurt, or you can *choose* to look to the God who loves you with all of His heart and accepts you and be healed.

Do not choose to be hurt any longer. Choose to receive healing and walk in loving acceptance by God through Jesus!

When David was healed from self-negativity and insecurity, he ended up being loved by the nation of Israel. When you choose to let yourself be loved and accepted by God, and then, you love and accept yourself, you are empowered by God. Soon, you will discover that others will love you as well.

The reason insecurity and self-negativity must be identified and removed from your life is because it keeps you from accessing the supernatural ability of God and keeps you bound to the earth.

> *The key to overcoming insecurity and self-negativity is to take your eyes off of you and focus instead on the love and acceptance of the Lord at all times!*

CHAPTER 23:

Miracles and the Glory

"to another the working of miracles, to another prophecy, to another discerning of spirits, to another different kinds of tongues, to another the interpretation of tongues."
1 Corinthians 12: 10 (NKJV)

The apostle Paul teaches us through the Holy Spirit that there is a gift called the working of miracles. Notice the Word of God is very clear that it is not called the gift of miracles but the gift *of the working* of miracles. That means that you must have the knowledge and the wisdom of God on what to think, believe, say, and do to cause the miracle to manifest in front of your eyes.

By the grace of God, in the name of Jesus, through the Holy Spirit, you can be used of the Lord to work the miraculous. Miracles can happen by your *faith*, through the *anointing*, or in the *Glory*. Faith, the anointing, and the Glory are different realms of God through Jesus Christ.

> **"Blessed be the God and the Father of our Lord Jesus Christ, who hath blessed us with all spiritual blessings in heavenly places in Christ;"**
> **Ephesians 1: 3 (KJV)**

In the original language, the *heavenlies* refers to territories, domains, and realms in Jesus Christ. It takes revelation of the Word of God to give you access to a realm in the Lord Jesus. The key to each realm in Christ is the revelation that opens up that realm by the grace of God.

For example, when a person hears the Word of God that Jesus is the Lord, that HE died on the cross for his OUR sins, was buried, and then three days later came back to life, he repents and believes. The realm of salvation opens up and Jesus becomes his Lord and SAVIOR.

> OF FAITH
> **"But what does it say? 'The word is near you, in your mouth and in your heart' (that is, the word of faith which we preach): that if you confess with your mouth the Lord Jesus and believe in your heart that God raised Him from the dead, you will be saved. For with the heart one believes unto righteousness, and with the mouth confession is made unto salvation."**
> **Romans 10: 8- 10 (NKJV)**

When a person acts on this revelation, the person is saved by the grace of God in Jesus. A person believes in his heart and confesses with his mouth the LORDSHIP of JESUS. His sins are forgiven, and now he stands before God justified (just as if he had never sinned), and he is saved. He has become a child of God.

In the very same way, a person hears the message that JESUS is a HEALER and a MIRACLE WORKER, and he receives that revelation. That revelation opens up the realm of healing and his disease disappears. He has a miracle by the goodness of God!

Revelation produces the manifestation!

When a person hears that Jesus is the baptizer in the Holy Spirit, believes that message and begins to speak in another tongue, you see the manifestation of the supernatural presence of God.

Once again, revelation determines the manifestation! Without a revelation you cannot enter the realm that Jesus has purchased for you, and that the Father offers you because of sacrifice and resurrection of Christ.

A person can minister in the area of miracles by the revelation of FAITH, the revelation of the ANOINTING, or the revelation of the GLORY.

The way a person administrates miracles in the realm of faith is not the same as it is in the realm of the anointing or the realm of the Glory. Each realm has revelations, a set of principles and systems,

that must be followed to bring the manifestation of the miraculous.

The Glory of God may be present in a service but unless you know the revelations and the guiding principles of that realm, and have the wisdom, knowledge, and understanding of how to manifest what is in that Glory, nothing will occur. You can only make it rain what is already present in the Glory. It takes revelation knowledge to know why the Glory is there. By the Word of the Lord, you learn the wisdom, the ways, and the workings of God to manifest miracles through the Glory.

All miracles are not the same.

> **"to another the working of miracles, to another prophecy, to another discerning of spirits, to another different kinds of tongues, to another the interpretation of tongues." 1 Corinthians 12: 10 (NKJV)**

There is the *gift of the working of miracles*.

> **"Then Peter said, 'Silver and gold I do not have, but what I do have I give to you: In the name of Jesus Christ of Nazareth, rise up and walk.'" Acts 3: 6 (NKJV)**

> **"saying, 'What shall we do to these men? For, indeed, that a notable miracle has been done through them is evident to all who dwell in Jerusalem, and we cannot deny it." Acts 4: 16 (NKJV)**

Here the Word of God gives a reference to *noteworthy miracles*. A religious leader is referring back to a miracle that occurred when Peter lifted up a man who had never walked in 40 years. The man was healed and began to praise God, walking and leaping! I believe that when the lame walk, the blind see, and the deaf hear, these are called noteworthy miracles!

> **"And Stephen, full of faith and power, did great wonders and signs among the people." Acts 6:8 (NKJV)**

The Greek word here for *signs* means miracles. The word *great* means *mega miracles*. Now this is a reference to either big miracles or many miracles. So now we have miracles, noteworthy miracles, and great miracles.

> **"God also bearing witness both with signs and wonders, with various miracles, and gifts of the Holy Spirit, according to His own will?" Hebrew 2:4 (NKJV)**

> **"God did extraordinary miracles through Paul," Acts 19:11 (NIV)**

These *extraordinary miracles* are miracles that are unprecedented, out of the ordinary, and unusual. These are miracles that had never been done before! There is no scripture for this kind of a miracle in terms of history.

There are also *different patterns* for the miraculous.

Let me refer you to the book of Exodus chapter three to show you one pattern. In the book of Exodus, the sons of Israel were in captivity and slavery. First, they began to cry out to God.

"Now it happened in the process of time that the king of Egypt died. Then the children of Israel groaned because of the bondage, and they cried out; ..." Exodus 2: 23 (NKJV)

Next, Moses began to hear from God.

"So when the Lord saw that he turned aside to look, God called to him from the midst of the bush and said, 'Moses, Moses!'" Exodus 3: 4 (NKJV)

Then, Moses begins to obey God.

"Now the Lord said to Moses in Midian, 'Go, return to Egypt; for all the men who sought your life are dead.' Then Moses took his wife and his sons and set them on a donkey, and he returned to the land of Egypt. And Moses took the rod of God in his hand." Exodus 4: 19-20 (NKJV)

Through the obedience of Moses there are signs, wonders, and miracles!

"So the Lord said to Moses: 'See, I have made you as God to Pharaoh, and Aaron your brother shall be your prophet. You shall speak all that I command you. And Aaron your brother shall tell Pharaoh to send the children of Israel out of his land. And I will harden Pharaoh's heart, and multiply My signs, and My wonders in the land of Egypt.'" Exodus 7: 1-3 (NKJV)

In order to move in the miraculous one pattern reveals four steps. Somebody cries out to God. Somebody hears God. The person who hears, obeys God. And then, you see the manifestation of the miraculous.

When you look at the ministry of JESUS, you can see that HE moved in the realms of faith, the anointing and the Glory.

> **"As soon as Jesus heard the word that was spoken, He said to the ruler of the synagogue, 'Do not be afraid; only believe.' And He permitted no one to follow Him except Peter, James, and John the brother of James." Mark 5: 36-37 (NKJV)"Then He took the child by the hand, and said to her, 'Talitha, cumi,' which is translated, 'Little girl, I say to you, arise.'" Mark 5:41 (NKJV)**

When the twelve-year-old girl died, Jesus said to the parents *only believe*. After that Jesus walked into the room where the dead girl was, told her to arise, and she came back to life. That miracle of resurrection came by the *realm of faith*.

Here Jesus raises somebody from the dead through *the gift of his anointing*.

> **"Then He came and touched the open coffin, and those who carried him stood still. And he said, 'Young man, I say to you, arise.'" Luke 7:14 (NKJV)**

Jesus stops the funeral of a young man whose mother had suffered a double loss. Her husband was already gone, and now, they carried out her dead son, her only son. The Lord Jesus never asked the woman if she had faith. HE just simply stopped the funeral, spoke to the young man, and said, "Young man, I say to you, arise," and the young man came back to life! Jesus gave the son to the mother. Because this woman had lost her husband and her only son, she had no means of support. This was a miracle by the mercy and grace of Jesus Christ. This miracle happened as a result of the anointing on the life of Jesus!

Then you see Jesus bring the dead to life *by the Glory*. Jesus does not lay hands on the person. HE simply speaks the Word and the dead come back to life.

> **"Jesus said to her, 'Did I not say to you that if you would believe you would see the glory of God? Then they took away the stone from the place where the dead man was lying. And Jesus lifted up his eyes and said, 'Father, I thank You that You have heard Me. And I know that You always hear Me, but because of the people who are standing by I said this, that they may believe that you sent Me.' Now when He had said these things, He cried with a loud voice, 'Lazarus, come forth!' And he who died came out bound hand and foot with graveclothes, and his face wrapped with a cloth. Jesus said to them, 'Loose him, and let him go.'" John 11: 40-44 (NKJV)**

This man who had been dead for four days comes back to life totally restored by the power and Glory of God.

Jesus took the little girl by the hand and brought her back to life. Jesus was standing over the young man when he brought him back from the dead. But Lazarus was in a tomb, a distance away from Jesus when He said, "Come forth". When the Glory of God is manifesting, what you speak comes to pass instantly or immediately. You do not even have to be physically present where the miracle happens because God will manifest Himself in the place where the miracle is needed, so that Jesus can be glorified!

Let me give you this testimony. I have been in services where all I did was *quote the Word of God* on healing, and many, many people were healed without me ever uttering a prayer for them. The Holy Spirit, the Glory of God manifested as soon as the Word was spoken and created miracles.

I have personally witnessed the manifest presence of the Lord come into a service, and when the Word is spoken, the blind see, the deaf hear, people get up out of wheelchairs and walk!

I have witnessed people lose weight supernaturally by the power and the Glory of God. One woman from Norway, who weighed herself before the church service, was touched by God and discovered that she had lost twenty pounds when the service was finished. One man in Missouri was not even seeking supernatural weight loss, but he was in the atmosphere of the miracles. When he got home from church, he discovered he had lost fifteen pounds. One woman in the state of

Texas literally lost fifty pounds in a church service. One man was touched by God. No hands were ever placed on him, and he lost one hundred pounds in two days because of the miracle Glory of Jesus!

One fourteen-year-old boy was totally blind in both eyes, and he received his sight without the laying on of hands because of the Glory power and presence of God!

I want to pray for you, right now. If you are in pain, put your hand where the pain is. In the name of Jesus, I speak to the spirit of disease in your body. I speak to the cause of the pain and the pain itself, and I command it to come out of your body! I command your body to be healed in the name of Jesus Christ right now! I command the pain and the reason for the pain to dissolve, die, disappear, fade away in Jesus's name for God's Glory! Be healed right now!

I want you to pay attention to how the pain begins to decrease. Watch it decrease until it is completely gone and your healing miracle manifests by the power and Glory of Jesus Christ.

If you are in need of supernatural weight loss, I want you to tell the Lord that you are repenting of your bad eating habits. Ask the Lord to forgive you right now. Get ready to begin to lose weight.

In the name of Jesus, I decree and declare supernatural weight loss happens in your body right now for the Father's Glory. I want you to praise God for the next twenty-five minutes, and then check yourself on your scale. Praise the Lord as HE has started doing the miraculous for you, in Jesus's name!

> **"You will also declare a thing, And it will be established for you; So light will shine on your ways." Job 22: 28 (NKJV)**

> **"For with God nothing will be impossible." Luke 1: 37 (NKJV)**

> **"But Jesus looked at them and said, 'With men it is impossible, but not with God; for with God all things are possible.'" Mark 10: 27 (NKJV)**

> **"Jesus said to him, 'If you can believe, all things are possible to him who believes.'" Mark 9:23 (NKJV)**

> **"Beloved, I wish above all things that thou mayest prosper and be in health, even as thy soul prospereth." 3 John 1:2 (KJV)**

In the original language what God is saying is this*: In every respect I want you to have a good journey in My will. I want you healed and healthy in your physical body. I want you to have a good journey and be healed and whole in your soul.*

Jesus wants to prosper in every area of your life. Jesus wants your mind healed! Jesus wants your body healed! Jesus purchased spiritual, mental, emotional, and physical healing for you! Take it! IT IS YOURS NOW! THE GLORY OF GOD AND POWER IS MAKING YOU WELL RIGHT NOW, IN JESUS'S NAME!

The key to the working of miracles is putting application to the revelation so that the promises of God can be manifested, in the name of Jesus!

CHAPTER 24:

Wisdom, Wealth, and the Glory

"And you shall remember the Lord your God, for it is He who gives you power to get wealth, that He may establish His covenant which He swore to your fathers, as it is this day." Deuteronomy 8:18 (NKJV)

"Can a person cheat God? Yet, you are cheating me! But you ask, 'How are we cheating you?' 'When you don't bring a tenth of your income and other contributions.' So a curse is on you because the whole nation is cheating me! 'Bring one-tenth of your income into the storehouse so that there may be food in my house. Test me in this way,' says the Lord of the Armies. 'See if I won't open the windows of heaven for you and flood you with blessings.'" Malachi 3: 8-10 (GW)

When a believer obeys the Word of God, gives tithes and offerings, and walks in the Spirit, the Glory of God can be released to bring financial blessing. The prophet, Malachi, says if you bring ten percent of your income to God and give liberally, that the Lord will open up to you the windows of heaven and pour you out a blessing.

Many people think all you have to do is give ten percent, give offerings to the church or to the minister, and that will cause you to have financial prosperity. But, let's examine what the scripture says.

First, God says, *See if I will not open to you the windows of heaven.* What is the function of a window? A window enables you to see out of where you are and see into where you want to go. A window is a revelation or an idea that God gives you so that you can have His wisdom to generate wealth. This is wealth that is not just for your family and your loved ones, but wealth that can be used to extend the Kingdom of God on this earth and further the work of Jesus Christ.

When you went to school, you were taught math, reading, science, and history, but you were never taught how to become wealthy. Are you aware that basically what you were taught was how to become an employee and to earn an income? And yet, the value of money is going down, and debt is increasing faster than the income you can earn.

Most Jewish people are entrepreneurs. They are creative, inventive, and innovative. They seem to gain advantages and prosper. They study the Old Testament scriptures, and they follow them to the degree that they can get wealth through the wisdom that is revealed there. A number of Jewish people start out as employees who are earning an income, but after a while they become self-employed. When you are self-employed, you work for yourself. However, the problem with being self-employed is that you pay more taxes, and you are basically doing pretty much everything yourself.

A small business owner is defined as having less than five hundred employees. A large business owner is one who has over five hundred employees. One moves from being self-employed to a small business or a large business owner. You now have people working for you and you are generating wealth. A number of Jewish people are self-employed or are small or large business owners and leaders.

Then, there are those persons who become investors. They have moved past earned income, being self-employed, and paying lots of taxes. They have moved beyond being a small business owner, or even a large business owner, and they have made decisions that cause money to work hard for them. In addition, they get really intelligent people to work for them and generate more and more and more income. They are no longer working hard for their money but through knowledge, wisdom, and understanding, they have people working hard for them generating more money.

Ninety percent of the world's billionaires have invested in real estate. Have you ever paid attention to the fact that there are multimillionaires and billionaires who have learned certain principles so that they know how *not* to pay any taxes? They seem to have a different mindset, skill set, and play by a whole different set of rules than the middle class or the poor.

When the Glory of God came into Moses's life, Moses gave the sons of Israel principles on wisdom and wealth. You can go nearly any place on earth and you will find Jewish people who follow the principles of wisdom given by the Glory of God through the teaching of Moses, and they will be rich and wealthy!

The revelation of wisdom and wealth came into Moses's life as he spent time in the face, the presence, and the Glory of God. I think it is time for the church to study the wisdom and principles of wealth that Jesus gave Moses so that we can come into greater finances by the person and the Glory of God!

Have you considered the possibility that when God spoke to Moses, He talked to him about the prophet, Abraham?

> **"The Lord had said to Abram, 'Go from your country, your people and your father's household to the land I will show you.'" Genesis 12: 1 (NIV)**

When God spoke to Abraham, HE basically said, *I have some real estate for you.*

Nothing has really changed. If you own the right real estate, wealth will come to you! There is a reason why certain individuals, when they get to a certain level of income, invest in real estate, rent out those properties, and make that real estate generate more wealth for them.

Because of Jesus, *you* can receive ideas, insights, and foresights on how to generate wealth by the wisdom of the Spirit, so that instead of *you* working hard, you can have *your money* working hard for you! You can enjoy life instead of trying to make a living!

> **"The Lord will open to you His good treasure, the heavens, to give rain to your land in its season, and to bless all the work of your hand. You shall lend to many nations, but you shall not borrow. And the Lord will make you the head and not the tail; you shall be above only, and not beneath, if you heed the commandments of the Lord your God, which I command you today, and are careful to observe them." Deuteronomy 28: 12-13 (NKJV)**

What is the revelation this scripture talking about? The Glory of God that came into the life of Moses was teaching us on how to have freedom. The person who has to "borrow" is not free. The person who is "beneath" has been taken captive by some degree of poverty. The person who is the "tail" is slaving away to make a living or to make ends meet.

The person who applies the wisdom and wealth principles that came from the Glory is the head. He is above. He lends. He is not beneath. He is not the tail. He does not have to borrow. He has a measure of freedom and can actually enjoy life because he follows the principles of the Glory of God!

Let me give you some testimonies of people who have received wisdom and are enjoying the wealth of Jesus.

These testimonies come from people who have lived in a small town of less than twenty thousand in the Midwest.

One person was making approximately thirty thousand dollars a year. Three years after he began to believe in the wisdom and wealth of Jesus, he was making at least ninety-five thousand dollars a year.

Another person was making about thirty-five thousand dollars a year. Two years later he was making at least one hundred thousand dollars a year.

Another individual went from earning twenty-five thousand dollars to thirty-five thousand dollars in two weeks. After that, he went to making seventy-five thousand dollars a year.

One man had been in prison for eight-and-a-half years. Within two years of his release, he was making one hundred thousand dollars a year. He gave his heart to Jesus and followed the wisdom and wealth principles of Jesus. Now he is getting richer and richer by the grace of God. He has also accepted the call of God into the ministry!

Another man who had spent twelve years in prison, gave his life to Jesus. Now he is making one hundred thousand dollars a year, and his wife is also making the same amount.

One man is more than a millionaire, just by following the wisdom and the wealth principles of Jesus.

There are so many other testimonies that I can give you that are the result of the Glory of God in a believer as they follow Jesus. The focus of these people's lives who are so blessed by God is not wealth. It is Jesus!

There are others who are even much more financially blessed then the ones that I have mentioned here. The point is: *What Jesus has done for others, HE can do for you!* The Father has an inheritance for you, but you must follow the wisdom and wealth principles of Jesus to receive it. Make sure you keep your focus on Jesus and the Father. Share your wealth and give to others by the love of God!

The key to wealth in the Glory is to follow the wisdom found in the Word of God, but most importantly, to love and focus on Jesus and the Father first!

About Tony Temp

An associate pastor for more than 20 years and a pastor to other pastors, Tony Kemp is a man driven by the passion for serving his Lord Jesus with all of his heart, his mind, and his soul.

A brilliant speaker thought provoker, author, mentor, pastor, and TV personality, Pastor Kemp is the founder of Tony Kemp Ministries, through which he impacts over 200 countries through international TV.

Pastor Kemp also runs the ACTS Group, an international network that includes ministers from various nations.

Drawing from the Word of God, he firmly believes and teaches that the presence of God is made manifest when believers put the principles of the Bible into practice alongside fasting and prayer. He wholeheartedly believes in God's ability to do signs, wonders, and miracles, even today, and his vision is to teach believers to fellowship with God and experience real intimacy with the Father, Jesus, and Holy Spirit.

A consummate author, he has developed and produced many teachings such as "The Principles of Supernatural Ministry," "The Priceless Gift of Grace," "Discovering your Identity," and Face to Face with God.

He has been married to Deborah for over 40 years, and they are blessed with one son Philip, his wife Sarah, four grandchildren, as well as many spiritual sons and daughters across the United States, where he travels extensively.

You can find Pastor Kemp on Facebook, YouTube, and www.TonyKemp.com.